Explorers

North & East Yorkshire

Edited by Vivien Linton

First published in Great Britain in 2009 by
Young Writers
Remus House
Coltsfoot Drive
Peterborough
PE2 9JX
Telephone: 01733 890066
Website: www.youngwriters.co.uk

Book Design by Spencer Hart
Illustrations by Ali Smith

SB ISBN 978-1-84924 302 5

Foreword

At Young Writers our defining aim is to promote an enjoyment of reading and writing amongst children and young adults. By giving aspiring poets the opportunity to see their work in print, their love of the written word as well as confidence in their own abilities has the chance to blossom.

Our latest competition Poetry Explorers was designed to introduce primary school children to the wonders of creative expression. They were given free reign to write on any theme and in any style, thus encouraging them to use and explore a variety of different poetic forms.

We are proud to present the resulting collection of regional anthologies which are an excellent showcase of young writing talent. With such a diverse range of entries received, the selection process was difficult yet very rewarding. From comical rhymes to poignant verses, there is plenty to entertain and inspire within these pages. We hope you agree that this collection bursting with imagination is one to treasure.

Contents

Great Smeaton Primary School, Northallerton

Hampsthwaite Primary School, Hampsthwaite

Kirkby & Great Broughton Primary School, Stokesley

Kirk Hammerton CE Prima-y School, York

Le Cateau Community Primary School, Catterick Garrison

Lord Deramore's Primary School, York

Markington CE Primary School, Harrogate

The Poems

Humpty Dumpty

Humpty Dumpty was an egg,
His wall broke fastly,
He cut his hand,
Then he became nasty.

No one could put him back again,
'Oh no!' said the little egg.
He wanted to try again,
He started to beg.

He closed his eyes,
They were gone.
He was scared,
He sang a song.

He closed his eyes again,
They were back.
The man said,
'I am Jack.'

He got some glue,
To fix the egg.
When they finished
They needed a nose peg.

'Oh no!' said the egg,
'Please can you fix me?
I'm not happy,
I look like a bee.'

'I will fix you,
Have my egg suit.'
'Thank you,' said Humpty.
'This suit is cute.'

Joe Cannon (7)

Arncliffe CE Primary School, Arncliffe

The Three Goats

As the three goats were having their lunch,
The little goat pleaded,
'Oh big goat, oh big goat, come on let's have a munch.'
'I'll wait here,' said the big goat.

'Oh we can't go there because of the troll.
We won't go yet.'
Off they went on a long roll.
Bang, bang - 'Who woke me?'

'Help, please, try my brother.'
The troll waited.
'Oh my, oh my, you're a lover.'
He waited for the next.

Trot-trot, 'Here I come,' said the big goat.
'Never!' screamed the troll.
'I will shred you into a coat.'
'Oh, will you?'

'You're going down!'
'Try then!'
He butted the troll and went round,
Then they lived happily ever after.

Kate Hirst (10)
Arncliffe CE Primary School, Arncliffe

Three Naughty Pigs

In the middle of the wood,
Lived three naughty pigs.
They acted very silly,
They squished poor mice like soft figs.

They came along with a trumpety-trump,
They made some houses out of different things.
Made from bricks, sticks and one even made of straw,
I do hope they don't think they're kings.

They bought a gun,
They had some cigs.
With the gun they had some fun,
I think they remembered, they were pigs.

They had mobile phones,
But they made a racket.
One lost his, it was so tragic,
Then one tried to track it.

They tried and tried,
Until they saw a wolf.
'Hey give it back!' they cried.
'Never in a million years,' and gulp!

Thomas Hall (10)

Arncliffe CE Primary School, Arncliffe

The Three Billy Goats Gruff

There was a troll
Getting annoyed by a midge.
There was a troll
Under a bridge.

There were three goats
Crossing the bridge.
The troll lost the midge
And hit a ridge.

The three Billy goats
Who crossed the bridge to the grass.
The three Billy goats
Saw the troll pass.

The troll rolled into the river
He never learned to swim.
He tried to swim
But then he lost a limb!

The troll
Didn't see them again.
The troll
Thought they were a pain.

Edward Patrick Lund (10)
Arncliffe CE Primary School, Arncliffe

Mythical Creatures

They creep around up in the night,
If you're not careful they will give you a bite!
They have hairy arms and a big fat head,
The problem is, they never go to bed.

They smell bad, a bit like you,
The next thing you know they're chewing at your shoe.
They wave their arms, wiggle their legs,
Some people think they eat dinosaur eggs.

They have small toes, a big fat belly,
You want to see it, it wiggles like jelly.
One time I met this terrifying group,
Forever I am stuck with this horrible troupe!

Fin Malley (10)
Arncliffe CE Primary School, Arncliffe

Humpty Dumpty

Humpty Dumpty sat on the wall
Eating his favourite bananas.
He tried to put the skins
Down the king's pyjamas.

He tried and tried till he filled his mouth
With rotten bananas.

The king got cross
His pants fell down.
He told his boss and he said,
'If he does that to me again, I'm going to frown!'

Hollie Harrison (7)
Arncliffe CE Primary School, Arncliffe

Border Collie

Hard worker
Big barker
Joy maker
Bone digger
Mud leaver
Field trudger
Tail wagger
Great comforter
Four legged
Fluffy haired.

Grace Cannon (10)
Arncliffe CE Primary School, Arncliffe

Feelings

F eelings happen every day
E very person is different
E veryone has lots of feelings
L ots of feelings can hurt you
I n friendship feelings are happy
N ot always are they happy but sometimes sad
G rowing feelings everywhere
S how your feelings to everyone.

Eve Cannon (9)
Arncliffe CE Primary School, Arncliffe

Planets

P lanets floating in space
L earning with every step
A ll around I can see stars
N o life at all
E arth is so small
T o this very day people are exploring
S pace, it is a big place.

Max Metcalfe (10)
Arncliffe CE Primary School, Arncliffe

The Three Little Pigs

In the middle of the woods
Were three little pigs,
They loved to play in the mud
And eat up all the twigs.

Kallum Battye (11)
Arncliffe CE Primary School, Arncliffe

The Frozen Deer

Out at the edge of a forest
where nippy Jack Frost
freezes the ground solid,
and turns the shimmering night sky
sparkling like crystals,
the frozen deer follow their shadows.
Deeper into the forest
their icy hooves
clip
and
clop.

At last the warm sun rises
over the silhouetted trees
colour-washing the sky
and heating up
the forest.
The hard frost melts.
Icicles drip.
The icy wind blazes.
When the frozen deer
appear
snuffling out of the trees.
Bring them here,
bring them here,
bring there here.

Jodie Lodge (8)
Austwick CE (VA) Primary School, Austwick

The Frozen Owl

Out at the edge of the wood
where cold winds
freeze the trees
and nobody ever goes,
in this desolate place,
under the shiny stars,
an owl is hopping
alone
on the rough path,
his sharp claws
dig
and
hop.

Here in a sheltered hole
at the heart of the wood,
the owl lands and swoops in
to find wool and feathers
soft as a duvet.
The owl starts snoozing
like a purring cat
in the old, safe oak
His quiet call,
Tu-whit-tu-whoo
Tu-whit-tu-whoo
Tu-whit-tu-whoo.

Samuel Ogden (9)
Austwick CE (VA) Primary School, Austwick

The Frozen Fox

Out in the middle of a wood
Where creamy snow falls softly
Like melting ice cream,
Twigs snap in icy winds
And icicles fall smashing
On the rock-frosty ground.
A frozen fox trembles all alone,
Like a stray puppy
At the edge of the frosted wood.
His paws thump and thump.

In his cosy burrow
Deep under the tremendous hill,
His furry fox family snuggle
Into their hot water bottle of fluffy hay,
Listening for the frozen father fox to return
Like rustling leaves outside.
And when he comes to the safe burrow,
Let him in,
Let him in,
Let him in . . .

Jordan Simpson (9)
Austwick CE (VA) Primary School, Austwick

What Is The Moon?

The moon is a silver Saracen sword
waiting in the dark of night, ready for assassination.

It is the Dark Knight's silver batarang
being thrown into the shadows of the night.

It is Captain Jack's curved silver sonic detractor
shining in a pitch-black room.

It is a glowing spaceship door
leading to extra-terrestrial life forms with unfriendly features . . .

It is a part of a furon UFO blast
travelling through the night to destroy all that we hold dear.

It is a crescent-shaped space station
orbiting around the Earth, sending and receiving messages.

It is an evolutionary spacecraft
travelling through the coal-black sky to start a new race of aliens.

It is a shiny telephone
sending a message across the universe . . .

Scott Christie (10)
Austwick CE (VA) Primary School, Austwick

What Is The Moon?

The moon is a yellow banana
in a dark fruit bowl.

It is a pink lily
buried in plain black soil.

It is a curled-up cat
asleep on a cream slated floor.

It is a slice of lemon
floating in a glass of Coke.

It is a flat pancake
cooked in a cast iron pan.

It is a curled-up snake
hiding in a cold black tank.

It is a shiny earring
in an African's ear.

It is a white boomerang
flying past a cloudy wall.

Jessica Davis (8)
Austwick CE (VA) Primary School, Austwick

Our Alphabetical Class

Adam is an action man, Amber P is arty,
Amber S adores apples and is a smarty.
Esmée is extreme and likes to explore,
Harry C is out of hand and hungry for more.
Honor has lots of hobbies and is healthy,
Holly is happy, helpful and hopes to be wealthy.
James C is jolly, Jordan jests with jokes,
James M is a jumble and loves jelly with Coke.
Jodie is just so keen on jivey jewellery,
Jessica is a jockey and likes jam for tea.
Jade is a jogger and like to jump around,
Lily is lively, Leanne leaps over the ground.
Oscar hates onions and often does what he ought,
Olen overturns and goes over the top in sports.
Reece is relaxed, Ryan is restful,
Scott is sometimes silly and stressful.
Tom is thoughtful and terrific at a tricky task,
U, V, W, X, Y and Z and that is all my class.

Amber Plumbridge (9)
Austwick CE (VA) Primary School, Austwick

What Is The Moon?

The moon is a shiny assassin's Samurai sword
in the dead of the night, poised, ready for attack.

The moon is a curved bolt of lightning
tearing the sky apart.

The moon is a slice of lemon
in a fizzy drink of Coca-Cola.

The moon is a white snowball
thrown through the night.

The moon is a bent goose neck
chopped on a black cutting board.

The moon is a gleaming brooch
pinned to a dark, warm jumper.

The moon is a woollen sheep
lying on darkened grass.

Olen Gray Gunn (9)
Austwick CE (VA) Primary School, Austwick

What Is The Moon?

The moon is a shiny clock
ticking out of time.

The moon is a silver football
being kicked into a pitch-black net.

The moon is a curled-up lamb
bleating for its mother in the night.

The moon is a hanging telephone
calling in space.

The moon is a bright golf ball
being driven into orbit.

The moon is a dazzling sword
flashing into war.

The moon is a silver shield
ready for battle.

James Middleton (9)
Austwick CE (VA) Primary School, Austwick

What Is The Moon?

The moon is a silver earring
hanging on an African woman's ear.

It is a lovely lemon
in the top of a glass of Coke.

It is a shiny brooch
pinned onto a warm, cosy jumper.

It is a sparkling hair clip
clipped into some dark, still hair.

It is a slithering snake
sliding curved beneath a coal-black stone.

It is a bent boomerang
zooming in the windy air.

Honor Jeffrey (7)
Austwick CE (VA) Primary School, Austwick

A Renga For The Seasons

Winter
Freezing sugar snow,
Piling high as thick as cars,
Blanketing iced ground.

Summer
Fiery sun burns skin,
Hot children play out all day,
Cool down with ice cream.

Oscar Jeffrey (9)
Austwick CE (VA) Primary School, Austwick

Our Alphabetical Class

Adam is active, Amber P is arty,
Amber S adores applies and loves to party.
Esmée is energetic and smart,
Honor has a very kind heart.
Holly likes horse riding, Harry R is hazardous,
Harry C adores dragons and making a fuss!
Jordan has green eyes and is a neat writer,
James M is fast, funny and quite a fighter.
James C just likes to jump and joke,
Lily love licking lollies and is lively with her folk.
Oscar likes octopus and playing out,
Reece races, riding round and about.
Sam is silly but can be swish,
Tom likes tasting tuna fish!

Harry Reid (8)
Austwick CE (VA) Primary School, Austwick

A Renga For The Seasons

Summer
Hot, burning summer, bright day,
Children play on toasting streets,
Birds sing lovely tunes.

Spring
Marshmallow blossom,
Coming out in warm sunshine,
Perfuming the air.

Amber Simpson (9)
Austwick CE (VA) Primary School, Austwick

A Renga For The Seasons

Summer
Hot as fire, sun burns
Bathers on boiled beaches
Cool down in calm sea.

Spring
Lamb born on a farm,
Eating grass with its mother.
Such a lovely spring.

Winter
Cold as frozen lakes.
Snows wildly in the winter.
Time to go to bed.

Jade Simpson (9)
Austwick CE (VA) Primary School, Austwick

A Snow Blanket

As snug as a soft blanket.
Clear, crystal-white
Camouflages the polar bear silky soft.
Fresh from the clear blue sky
The cosy blanket surrounds him
As he snoozes in the warm, cuddly blanket
In the daylight.
The camouflage protects him
From the dark winter's night.
So little Polar Bear cuddles up tight.

Rebecca Billings (10)
Broomfield School, Northallerton

Call Of The Rainforest

The rainforest was calling,
calling to the ground.

Wiggling worms, rusty-coloured roots
the weight of the rainforest crushing down
like a million tonnes of rock
they all hurt me, hurt me, hurt me.

The rainforest was calling,
calling to the trees.

Mischievous monkeys, blubbering beetles,
chirruping chinchillas, offensive owls,
twittering toucans and acting anacondas,
all in my branches they go slithering,
crawling, flying, climbing, living in me, the tree.

The rainforest was calling,
calling to the people.

Two-legs coming, chopping, killing, oh no more two-legs coming,
but two-legs stop chopping, killing; chopping, killing.
two-legs go away, away.

The rainforest was calling,
calling to the dead forest.

Slowly the forest, recovers, recovers and the animals return
muttering moths, vaccinating vipers, calling kingfishers,
crunching catfish, the rainforest is coming alive again.

Asa Dant (10)
Broomfield School, Northallerton

The Worst Days Of The Week

On Monday when I go to school,
I know that I won't break the rule,
Cos when I'm going across the road,
I'll be sure to use the Green Cross Code.

The Green Cross Code
The Green cross code,
When I'm walking over the road,
I will use the Green Cross Code.

On Tuesday I saw a girl,
Who really badly had to curl,
Because she walked out into the road,
And never used the Green Cross Code.

The Green Cross Code,
The Green Cross Code,
When you're crossing the road,
Use the Green Cross Code.

On Wednesday there was a boy,
Who ran out to get a toy,
His safety jacket never shone,
Because of that now he is gone.

The Green Cross Code,
The Green Cross Code,
If you don't want to be hit on the road,
Use the Green Cross Code.

On Thursday I was playing with my friend,
The ball rolled out, I thought it was the end.
He stopped when he saw the car,
It's a good job it wasn't going far.

The Green Cross Code,
The Green Cross Code,
If you want to be safe,
Use the Green Cross Code.

On Friday my brother was out,
He said that he would be back without a doubt.
He walked out into the road,
And the car that was coming never slowed.

The Green Cross Code,
The Green Cross Code,
Always use the Green Cross Code,
The Green Cross Code.

Courtney Elsworth (10)
Broomfield School, Northallerton

Ride Safe

While on your speedy bike
Wear fluorescent clothes all nice and bright.
They're cool,
So don't be a fool.

I'll tell you a story about a boy named Mike,
He had a terrible accident falling off his bike.
He had a helmet on and a bicycle light
But didn't dress all safe and bright.
Only dark clothes which weren't safe
When the car hit him, he landed on the pavement face.

His body was battered - blood on his cheek
He was very, very, very weak.
The driver shocked at his state
Rushed him to the hospital but it was too late.

So learn from Mike's mistake
Don't leave it too late
Or you might suffer the same fate!

Osaremen Irianan (11)
Broomfield School, Northallerton

Lucky This Time

I walk along peacefully,
Staring at the sky.
Trudging through old leaves,
Watching the world go by.

The crossing's further down the road,
It'll make me late for school.
Should I get delayed,
Or disobey the rule?

I look right, I look left,
There're no cars at all.
I run straight into the road,
I trip on my bag and fall.

A squeal of brakes,
A flash of lights,
A beep of a horn.
But there's no going back.
A bang on the head,
And it all goes black.

I wake up in hospital,
In a lot of pain.
I got lucky this time,
I'll never do it again.

Rachael Webb (10)
Broomfield School, Northallerton

Ruling Rainforest

What's that I hear?
Running rivers,
Scuttling spiders,
Rambling ocelot,
Scrambling, scaly lizards.

What's that I feel?
Stabbing thorns,
Digging tapir, noses in my roots,
Life below,
Wailing wind.

What's that I see?
Drumming raindrops hitting the ground,
Big skeletons stretching their arms,
Deep dug holes,
Scary grubs.

What's that I smell,
Damp, cool air rising up my nose,
My eyes watering with the dung below,
Tropical breezes blowing,
Hot, dry air tearing through the skies.

My leaves are falling all around,
I am gone to the ground.

Holly Austin (11)
Broomfield School, Northallerton

The Rainforest

The groaning ground sees
Winking tree knots as it ripples around,
The ancient animals stampeding
Squishing the young yams.

The wash-out waves eating
Mangled mangos and pulverised papaya,
The tangled tapir gets caught
In the receding reeds.

I waddle through the rainforest
Winking back to the tree knots,
The anteaters twirling their noses
Through the ants' alcove.

The stretching tree roots
Curling through the undergrowth,
The roaring waterfall
Destroyed the kiwis' kingdom.

The wailing wallows
Getting beaten by the
Macho manatee.

Liam Grant (11)
Broomfield School, Northallerton

The Sound Of The Rainforest

Croaking grasshoppers get louder and louder,
Crackling branches on the ground,
Snoring sloths hanging from the trees,
This is the sound of the rainforest.

Singing tribesman in the distance,
Calling marmosets up above,
Bristling leaves silhouetting downwards,
This is the sound of the rainforest.

Stamping tapirs breaking twigs,
Rushing water getting faster and faster,
Splashing fish getting dragged in the currents,
This is the sound of the rainforest.

Dripping water flowing from tree to tree,
Crashing trees chopped away,
But now the sound is broken by chainsaws ringing
And motors revving.

Every day the rainforest gets loud, louder,
Louder and louder.

James Martin (11)
Broomfield School, Northallerton

Catfish

I am the hunter of the deep
On living prey I feed
Though sometimes now and again
Rotten wood is a treat.

Food that for some reason
Wriggles as it goes down
Death rolls tell me
Stories of howling tides

But up there no gills rule all
Wood poisoners, fish choke in their nets
Fur on their heads and two legs
Oh what is that hook in front?

I take the bait, *argh!* Death, pain,
The surface comes down, pain, pain
No, gill sharps cut me up, pain

They rip out my life, no gills!

George Fox (10)
Broomfield School, Northallerton

The Snow Blanket

Snow blanket settles calmly on the polar bear,
Soft and cosy,
Warmer than Arctic sun.
Comfy blanket,
Smoother than silk.
It is fresh and pure as water.

Matthew Mason (10)
Broomfield School, Northallerton

Sounds Of The Rainforests

The rainforest was calling,
The rhythmic beat of rain,
The gushing waterfall,
Yodelling tribes.

Silently stalking jaguars,
Fuming, shouting rivers,
Whistling branches,
The squealing kill of an ocelot.

The pulsating of the ground,
The beat of a stampede,
The laughter of the trees,
The deep voices of the rocks.

The gurgling of a drinking animal,
The hissing of a snake,
The chomping of a squirrel monkey,
Then all is silent as the woodcutters come.

Ewan Cameron (11)
Broomfield School, Northallerton

The River Amazon

I'm running through the rainforest: what do I see?
A rocky pathway ahead of me, full of surprises.
Slimy snakes slithering around
Grasshoppers hopping on the forest floor.

I'm running through the rainforest: what do I feel?
Raindrops falling all of the time.
Fish are flowing through me
As they dash to reach their destination.

I'm running through the rainforest: what do I hear?
I can hear the muttering of the ticklish tapir,
Rustling in the grass, rustling in the grass,
It must be the grasshoppers fighting for lunch.

I am the river Amazon . . .
The explorers search me for treasures,
But sometimes just find weird creatures.
The River Amazon, the River Amazon.

Liam Harrison (10)
Broomfield School, Northallerton

The Acacia Tree

My leaves crunch to the ground,
I rock around in the awful storm,
And shade myself in the hottest days,
I am the tallest of all my people.

I peer down to the animals passing,
Jaguar, tapir, capybara and sloth,
Ocelot sometimes biting my toenails,
I am creaky because I'm quite old.

The squirrel monkey tries to make a nest in my hair,
The blue morphio caterpillar tickles me,
The Amahuaca tribesman steals some of my skin,
That pesky fern tree leans against my legs.

I tower over anyone or anything,
No one dare backchat to me,
Everyone knows where I live
The Amazon Rainforest is the place.

Lucy Barker (11)
Broomfield School, Northallerton

I Am A Tree

I am a tree,
Rain splashes,
Wind blows,
I shiver, but no one can see me.

I am a tree,
Grasshoppers stamp painfully,
Sloths pull on my branches,
I shake, but no one can feel me.

I am a tree,
Tribesmen carve my wood,
I bleed and bleed,
I howl, but no one can hear me.

I am a tree,
Nobody listens, nobody cares,
Nobody asks my opinions,
Nobody knows I'm here.

Maya Dorling (11)
Broomfield School, Northallerton

The Rainforest Kingdom

In the rainforest a kingdom lies,
Where green giants stretch their arms,
Rainbow wings dance and parade,
Monkeys dart through the trees.

Here he comes, the jaguar,
Pounding on the soft forest floor,
Delicate orchids hang on twisted branches,
Tickling his great spotted fur.

Sapphire butterflies dart through the sky,
Insect armies invade lush, emerald leaves.
Wriggling roots cover the vast animal kingdom,
They are snakes stalking the carpet below.

In the rainforest a kingdom lies,
Where monkeys howl as they swing,
A bird's melody echoes through the branches,
The wind whispering goodbye.

Becky Raper (10)
Broomfield School, Northallerton

The Seat Belt

Wear your seat belt in the car,
Or you'll end up as dead as tar.
Wear your seat belt in the car,
Don't be stupid and you'll go far.

Wear your seat belt in the car,
Even if you're not travelling far.
Wear your seat belt in the car,
Or you'll end up in the tar.

Wear your seat belt on the bus,
Then you'll end up home in time for couscous.
Wear your seat belt on the bus,
Then you'll live, just like us.

Wear your seat belt all the time,
Then that will cover all the crime.
Wear your seat belt all the time,
I hope you enjoyed this little rhyme.

Jake Foster (10)
Broomfield School, Northallerton

The Snow-White Blanket

The white, fresh blanket settled on the polar bear.
The crisp, crystal-white wind protector
Covered the small polar bear as it sank deeper
Into the blanket of white.

The cotton wool blanket stays there
Like fur on Santa's coat,
Warm,
Comfy.
Polar Bear is safe from cruel wind and rain.

The polar bear slumbered,
The blanket stayed,
Protecting.
Giving heat, growing more every second.

Hannah Tretheway (10)
Broomfield School, Northallerton

The Snow Blanket

The polar bear lay
Covered
With a thick, crystal-white blanket.
It shines in the sun,
Camouflages the bear with its look.
Smooth and soft, warming its owner.
Plain colour makes the blanket impossible to find.
Blanket's fluffy texture comforts the bear while it sleeps.

Avi Kumar (9)
Broomfield School, Northallerton

The Forest Floor

I feel pain as I am in shame
I see rain but it feels like grain,
I groan and I moan when the light shines on me
But I cannot see, unfortunately.

I cry as I look up to the sky
Tired of being trampled on
Sick of snakes slithering over me
I'm stroppy when I'm sleepy.

I am the forest floor and wish for more
I'm sore when the trees press on me
I hear drumming raindrops falling
I am the forest floor but wish for more!

Daniel Tarren (11)
Broomfield School, Northallerton

Snow Blanket

The snow blanket settled,
Its smooth layer covering fully.
It was so silky, warm and clean.
A snug, soft, cosy cover.
Its fresh new smell all over
The polar bear inside.
The snow blanket had settled.

Jessica Logan (9)
Broomfield School, Northallerton

Polar Bear Poem

The crystal-white snow gently fell on the polar bear's back
Through the night,
A blanket,
Covering the surface of the polar bear,
Fluffy, opaque, layer,
Cosy, but cold on top.

Fresh, white blanket
Camouflaging him from the harsh world.
The velvety blanket covered the top layer.
A streamline of silver glimmering in the sunlight
Caught everything's eye.
The slumbering polar bear woke up.

Anna Readman (10)
Broomfield School, Northallerton

The Polar Bear's Blanket

The polar bear's blanket,
Smooth and warm, although cold.
Clean and cosy, white and washed,
Covers him softly through the cold winter's night.
Warm underneath with a soft surface.
White and fluffy, keeps him warm.

Curling up with an opaque blanket,
He will rest all night
On the blanket washed and clean,
His blanket lies there through the deep, dark night.
Later the blanket is washed with a warm shower.

Matthew Williams (10)
Broomfield School, Northallerton

The Blanket Of Snow

The snow, a sparkling, soft, snugly blanket,
Its crystal-white camouflages the polar bear,
Making him warm and safe.
The silky blanket wrapped around him,
Keeping the warmth in and the wind out,
Like a friend fighting the wind to keep him cosy.
Its smooth texture settles him down like a soft cloud.

Amelia Grayson (10)
Broomfield School, Northallerton

The Snow Blanket

The blanket of snow settled on the polar bear,
covering it, never stopping.
Cold but cosy warm underneath, completely white.
Smoothly covering the whole bear.
Safely snoozing in a soft cloud.
Blanket washed, fresh and clean snow still piling on.
So opaque you cannot see the polar bear at all.

Jasmin Darbyshire (9)
Broomfield School, Northallerton

The Beach

Here we come to the wonderful beach,
Everything seems as delicious as a peach.
The children playing in the transparent sea,
Adults sitting on the yellow sand, being as kind as can be.

All you can see is:
Children splashing,
Adults sitting,
Toddlers walking,
Teenagers running,
Grandads moaning
And grandmas laughing.

All you can hear is:
Children banging
And babies crying.
You cannot move as it is as crammed as a train.

Adults are always sweating at the beach.
All you can hear is:
Music booming,
Hearts beating,
And children sobbing at the fabulous beach.

At the beach all you want to touch is
Fish and chips
In your mouth they're very mouth-watering and yummy.
All you can taste is:
Fish and chips,
Fizzy drinks,
Popcorn crunching
And candyfloss
At the fabulous beach.

Tyrone Warhurst (10)
Dorchester Primary School, Hull

Gemma's Dance Academy

I walk through the ancient doors,
Seeing the shimmering checked floors.
With great big green handles,
Wishing I'd come in my sandals,
To be able to slip and dance
For I have a chance
To become a professional dancer.
In Gemma's Dance Academy.

Slip,
Slide,
Fall,
Bang,
Click,
Crunch,
Straight leg!
In Gemma's Dance Academy.

Warm up,
Get a cup of water
They taught her
For when they get hotter,
Hot,
Tired,
You're fired!
Shake a leg!
Get up!
You're tough!

In Gemma's Dance Academy:
Feet banging,
People sighing,
Everyone cooling down
With a little frown!
Scream,
Cheer,
Bang,

Racket,
A packet of crisps,
Loud music!
In Gemma's Dance Academy.

Plain water,
There's nothing to taste,
Now they're pulling a grumpy, moody face,
For now they're tired,
Finally they've hired
A new drinks machine
And she's seen
It's time to go home!
In Gemma's Dance Academy.

Rush,
Push,
Bang car door,
Lazy head,
Everyone treads
To bed
No sound at home
Away from
Gemma's Dance Academy.

Hannah Dusher (10)
Dorchester Primary School, Hull

Going To The Airport

Are we nearly there yet?
Oh I forgot, we are still at the service station.
I can see a wind turbine.
Ha-ha, I saw it first.

Oyoy, I'm hungry!
I know I should have eaten but I wasn't hungry then.
Have you got any mints?
Oh, you've got some crisps,
Have you got any salt and vinegar?
You do?
I want them.

I'm bored.
Hey, I've thought of a great game of Horrid Henry.
OK. I'll go first.
Super Sam.
What do you mean evil Oyoy?
You are not evil,
It's also not right, it has to be O and O.

Ah, where did Sophie come from?
Honestly that dog.
She's always doing tricks.
Anyway, where did she come from?
Oh I see, Grandad.
Did you check the boot before we left?
Well, we've got a suitcase problem!

Sam Gardiner (10)
Dorchester Primary School, Hull

The Toilet Excuse

'Miss, Miss, toilet! I - I need the toilet, I'm bursting.
Do you want me to pee my pants?
You do?
What?

Ha, ha! Right in the head.
I'm flicking here, flicking there,
I'm flicking nearly everywhere.
Sorry Miss, now back to flicking the rubber!

Ouch! Who flicked Me?
Argh! It hurts.
Attack of the rubbers, take cover.
I've had enough of this, time to fight back.
Eat rubber!
Yes, I know this is the second time in one minute
That I've got in trouble.
Sorry Miss, but I - I need the toilet.

I'm so bored. Aha, time for a little sing-song.
Little Miss Muffett sat on a tuffet,
The poor little spider lay chewed-up inside her.
Ha, ha, ha!
Oi, Jolly Jake, Helpful Hannah, Cool Cain, over here!
Hello, I have to get out of here.
Miss, Miss, I need the toilet!'

Ellis Atkinson (10)
Dorchester Primary School, Hull

Sticky, Sweet Haunted House

As I walked into the creepy, creaky haunted house
With the horrible ancient doors,
I felt so frightened and I could smell the fear
And see blurry things like ghosts
And even spookier, flying teapots!
I wanted to shout help but I slowly and quietly walked up
the creepy stairs and could hear:
Ghosts shouting, 'Boo!'
Witches cackling,
Me running,
People screaming,
Vampires scaring,
At the sticky, sweet haunted house.
I was feeling horrible, even worse, let me tell you:
Sad,
Scared,
Frightened,
At the sticky, sweet haunted house.

Then I thought I had to shout it,
But no, I was feeling a little more brave now.
I was thinking it, but instead I held it and I shouted@
Arrgghh!
At the sticky, sweet haunted house.

Oliva Hultum (9)
Dorchester Primary School, Hull

Line Up

'Right Class 6, there goes the fire alarm. Let's line up.
Twiggy, I said line up. Oh, you're desperate.
Well you can't got to the toilet if there's a real fire, can you?
Yes, well that's too bad.
What? You have permission from Miss Pelly?
Go then!
Yes, Pierce, well we need to line up, because we need to
stay calm.
Harry, don't run and scream at the fire alarm!
Well, we need to stay calm and not scare anyone.
Butch, don't cry. Butch, it's a test. Butch, never mind.
Curly, what's the matter? You need to finish your work?
That's a shame because the fire alarm has gone off.
Oh, Miss Pelly, yes we know we should be outside but
Curly has to finish his work.
Oh, I didn't mean to make you upset, Miss Pelly.
What Pierce? I am the meanest teacher in the world?
No you didn't say that, but it's true.
Yes Goose, you need to call Pecko. Well Pecko is right next to you.
Why not talk to her?
Finally we're outside.
Roscoe, no turtle baseball hat!'

Abigail Davison (10)
Dorchester Primary School, Hull

Campsite

As you arrive at the campsite,
You can see people making cooked breakfast.
I can smell the fatty, salty bacon
And the sizzling sausages on the grill.

I can hear people's dogs barking
And their music booming.
People screaming
And the sun beaming.

I can feel the wet grass underneath the silky tent
And I can feel the bumpy blow-up bed underneath me.
The quilt getting warm as I put the little heating box on.

When I take my lid off the fizzy Fanta,
It all explodes onto the floor
And now it's only half full,
At the campsite!

When it's time to go home, we pack our tent up
Then drive onto the roads.
By the time we reach the roads
I'm already asleep.
Night, night!

Thalia Slade (9)
Dorchester Primary School, Hull

Less Talk

'Right Class 8,
Has everybody brought their homework?

Martyn, what do you mean you forgot?
You left it at school!
Suessy, you can't go to the toilet, because last time
You bunged them up and nobody could go for months!
Ahh, Mrs Liddle, do you like this lovely class?
No?
Would that be because half the class are not in school uniform?
I thought so.
Bob, your homework please.
Your dog ate it?
And Mercy, you granny chucked it in the fire to get warm?
Really, I do find that hard to believe.

Class 8,
Right now, whoever hasn't brought their homework is staying in.
Now can we get on with complex sentences?
No Jake, sentences, not dentists!'

Billy Hall (10)
Dorchester Primary School, Hull

Fun Alarm

'Right Class 9, let's do the register.
Max, stop hitting Linda!
Martin stop throwing rulers!
Someone give me the register. Oh no, the fire alarm's gone.
Off, quick everyone line up!
Martin, stop hiding behind the chairs and come and line up
or you'll be left inside.
Right now everyone, come outside!
Pardon? What do you mean, you have no shoes on?
What have I told you?
Everyone, stop shouting so I know that everyone is here.
What do you mean, Martin is still inside?
Mr Reynold, can you go and get Martin for me?
Martin, you naughty boy, you had me worried sick.
No Martin, I wasn't actually sick,
You made me feel sick.
Well, at least you're out now!'

Luke Tweddle (9)
Dorchester Primary School, Hull

Holiday Time At Haven

As you get out the car,
You will hear the birds singing.
When you get inside you will be
Overwhelmed by the smell of the chocolate bar.
The site is crowded,
Children are screaming,
Parents are yelling.
On the way around the children are moaning
Parents are groaning.
Time to go
Dirty key to give back.
Jump inside,
Feeling glum
Ignite the engine.
Slip into your dream.

Cain Smith (10)
Dorchester Primary School, Hull

Eastfield!

E xciting trips, we get to go on.
A lways try your best, that is what we do.
S ATs in Year 6, tricky or not.
T eachers drinking tea, while they teach us English.
F un, we can have, only if we work hard.
I s it time for maths, PE or art?
E veryone having fun, it's near the end of term.
L ots of different plays, from each and every year.
D id you enjoy your time? We will see you all next year!

Millie Dorkin (11)
Eastfield Primary School, Hull

I Go Shopping

I go shopping with my mum
We usually buy:

Buns for me,
Bread for sandwiches,
Milk for breakfast,
And lots more.

I go shopping with my mum
We usually buy:

Beans with fish,
Peas with chicken,
Hotdogs with sauce,
And lots more.

I go shopping with my mum
We usually buy:

Potatoes for chips,
Carrots for Sunday dinner,
Sprouts for Christmas
And lots more.

I go shopping with my mum
But when it's my birthday, we buy:

Birthday cake,
Ice cream,
Candles,
And lots more
And all for me!

Courtney Sleight (9)
Eastfield Primary School, Hull

Birthday Party!

Happy birthday!

Knock, knock!
Come on inside
Join the party
Shout out your name
You never know
You might win some games!

Knock, knock!
Happy birthday! Hello Soph!
Come on in
Join the party
Have some fun
You never know
You might get chocolate buns!

Knock, knock!
Happy Birthday! Hello Court!
Come on in
Join the party
Don't be shy
You never know
You might laugh till you cry!

Happy birthday!

Leanne Day (10)
Eastfield Primary School, Hull

I Wish

I wish I had a dog,
I wish I had a brother,
I wish I had an aircraft
On which I would hover.

I wish I could be queen,
I wish I could be a hippie,
I wish I had a make-up box
With loads and loads of lippy.

I want to live on Mars,
I want to be eighteen,
I want to live in a mansion,
Cos I'm really, really keen.

I wish I had everything
In the whole wide world
But we both know it's not gonna happen
Cos I'm only a little girl.

Robyn Everett (11)
Eastfield Primary School, Hull

The Sea

T he sea clashes against the rocks.
H idden in the deepest, darkest caves.
E nd the day with a splash.

S ea is silent, wet and cold.
E veryone will see you tomorrow.
A bit of fun to come.

Shona Rae Dows (10)
Eastfield Primary School, Hull

Night-Time

When night is dark
Where swooping bats lark
Run as fast as you can!

When bones rattle on the floor
Skeletons are knocking at your door
Don't answer it at all!

When the full moon is out
And monsters are creeping about
Stay as still as a statue!

When ravenous wolves howl
When scary creatures growl
Stay away, stay away!

When night is dark
Where swooping bats lark
Run as fast as you can!

Ellie Tuttle (10)
Eastfield Primary School, Hull

Penguins

P enguins are really cute
E ven thought they can't fly
N ever hurt pengu ns
G o to Antarctica to see them
U nusual penguins eat shellfish
I like penguins a ot
N ever kill penguins.

Callum Gill (10)
Eastfield Primary School, Hull

Celebrations, Celebrations

Celebrations, celebrations through the year,
Christmas presents, toys and fun.

Celebrations, celebrations,
Easter bunnies, chocolate eggs and fun.

Celebrations, celebrations,
Valentine's Day, hearts, flowers, love and fun.

Celebrations, celebrations,
Mums' and Dads' Day, breakfast, cards and fun.

Celebrations, celebrations,
Weddings, rings, cakes and fun.

Celebrations, celebration,
Christenings, water, babies, vicars and fun.

Celebrations are always fun!

Chloe Whitney (9)
Eastfield Primary School, Hull

Lemurs

So cute and cuddly
Lemurs are always there
They're so lovely
And have thick fur.

They all travel in packs
Even in rain
Like fierce stray cats
They're never in pain.

Gregory Parrott (10)
Eastfield Primary School, Hull

Wakey-Wakey

Excuse me for a sec
I'm just getting dressed
To go swimming with my friends.

At half past ten I'm coming back
To wash my hair
And have a bath.

At twelve o'clock
You'll never guess what,
I'm going ice skating too.

And just then I heard a voice,
'I thought you were out ice skating
not resting, you sleepyhead!'

Oh! It was my mum!

Beathany Barwell (10)
Eastfield Primary School, Hull

Moonlight

M oonlight is a gorgeous sight,
O bviously shining bright,
O ver all it's so light,
N ever ever any dimmer,
L ight from the moon is glimmering at night,
I f clouds cover it it makes another gorgeous sight,
G lowing bright every second of the night,
H ighlights in my hair,
T winkling stars shining above.

Claire Batty (10)
Eastfield Primary School, Hull

Waves

W aves washing up the golden shore
A nchor chains snapped by the muscular water
V ehicles on the cliffs with their caravans burning
E verybody in the sea swimming while it's blistering
S ome people surfing in the salted water.

S eagulls swifting in the air
P eople bathing on the beach
L eeches sucking on a man's toe
A rrogant fish biting people
S ushi is made out of fish
H owling people running across the sand
I njured people who have been attacked by sharks
N ames being called for help!
G ames being played on the beach.

Ryan Burgin (10)
Eastfield Primary School, Hull

My Best Friend

Have you ever had a friend who plays with you,
Does your nails or pillow fights too?
To mess around or go to town
Or cheers you up when you are down?

Who feeds your rabbit when you're away?
Then one day, she had to say,
'I'm going now, I'm going today . . . '
I'm so sorry she has moved far away.

Shaan Kaur (10)
Eastfield Primary School, Hull

Isra And The Monkey

(In the style of Ogden Nash)

Isra met a silly monkey
Isra, Isra, looked quite funky
The monkey saw a banana, and with a quick glance,
It jumped up with joy and started to dance.
The first thing Isra knew, the banana was in her hand,
The next thing she knew, the monkey flicked a band!
Isra was angry and went to see
Where was that silly monkey?
The monkey leapt into Isra's arms . . .
(silly monkey!)
Isra didn't scream or scurry
she held it tight . . .
and took it to the farm in a hurry.

Isra Malik (10)
Eastfield Primary School, Hull

Hull City

H ull City playing on Saturday
U nder your cover watch telly
L ive with sports after you pulled down your sheets
L ife in Hull, it's a dream.

C ity centre is fun
I ll people in bed
T ell someone about the match
Y es watch the match!

Brendan Hookem (10)
Eastfield Primary School, Hull

Party

Everybody get your mobiles,
Everybody get your shoes,
Everybody get your party on,
'Cause I really wanna make you move.

Everyone has a friend,
Everyone makes it last,
Everyone get your groove on,
To make the party last.

Come on let's move,
To get some groove,
Everyone together now
Bring your light out of the dark.

So come on - do it now!

Chloe Louise Greaves (11)
Eastfield Primary School, Hull

The Ocean

Oceans foamy, long and wide,
Fast and furious all the time.
Sparkly white by the tide,
Get your swimming kit, now let's go slide.

Corals under the nice blues,
Boats going by, that's when I see you
And while the sea sleeps
The seaweed still creeps.

Georgie Perry (10)
Eastfield Primary School, Hull

I Wish

I wish I could fly in the sky
Whilst eating my favourite cherry pie.

I wish my dad didn't wear his hideous bow
He thinks he's a soldier standing in a row.

I wish I could be selfish and eat all the ice cream
But then my mum would just scream!

I wish I could go to the moon
Fly up there with a big balloon.

I wish my brother wasn't rude
But he is still in a mood.

I wish my wishes would come true
If they do I will give them to you!

Laura Howell (10)
Eastfield Primary School, Hull

Friendship

If you fall,
I'll catch you.
If you hurt yourself,
I'll get you a plaster,
And when you feel sick and down,
I'll help you up
And do the best I can to make you well.
'Why?' you say.
'Because I'm your friend
and always will be!'

Lydia Shaw (11)
Eastfield Primary School, Hull

I Help The World!

I help the world by:

Giving water to the Africans,
Giving homes to homeless people,
Giving toys to the children,
Giving life to animals that have been killed,
Giving money to the poor,
Giving food to the starving,
Giving families to children,
Giving love to the world,
Giving schools for kids to go to,
Giving blind people the power to see,
Giving deaf people the power to hear,

Who am I? . . . Jesus.

Ryan Lo (10)
Eastfield Primary School, Hull

When I Am Bored, I Count Things

When I am bored, I count things:
Rabbits, horses,
White vans speeding past,
Daisies, roses,
Bricks, cement markings,
Notes in my drum book,
Buttons on my remote,
My noisy
Heavy footsteps.
When I am bored, I count things.

Kai Mills (10)
Eastfield Primary School, Hull

Swimming

Swimming is fun,
Swimming is great,
Especially when you go with your mate!

Go on the slide,
With your friends,
The fun really never ends.
Play with the toys,
The balls, the foam,
I'm having fun.
'I don't want to go home!'

Swimming is fun,
Swimming is great,
Especially when you go with your mate!

Megan Kemp (10)
Eastfield Primary School, Hull

Teachers

T o school I go
E very day, except Saturday and Sunday
A pple for teachers
C akes, give to my teacher
H alley, that's her name
E xtremely nice
R osy red cheeks
S pecial, my teacher is!

Georgina Evelyn Reeve (11)
Eastfield Primary School, Hull

Roses Are Red

Roses are red,
Violets are blue,
Nothing is worse
Than taking drugs.

Roses are red,
Violets are blue,
Nothing is worse
Than smoking.

Roses are red,
Violets are blue,
Nothing is worse
Than seeing graffiti.

Connor Jenman (11)
Eastfield Primary School, Hull

Look At Me!

Look at me, look at me
I'm always gonna be . . . the best!
Look at me, look at me
Never will I be . . . the worst dressed!
Look at me, look at me
The sparkle . . . in my eye!
Look at me, look at me
My talent . . . will never die!
Look at me,
You have to see
That fame has always been in me!

Jasmine Hunte (10)
Eastfield Primary School, Hull

Cats And Dogs

C ats are howling, miaowing and scratching,
A nyone help them, give them a home.
T ake a cat or a dog
S o don't wait, come and get them!

A nd they are waiting for someone,
N o one can deny that you love them.
D on't forget they can be fun and not bad.

D ogs and cats are lovable pets,
O utside they run and play.
G et a new best friend today,
S pend lots of time with your new pet.

Conor Sheldrick (11)
Eastfield Primary School, Hull

Flicky My Dog

F licky my dog
L icks my face
I love her
C are for her
K issed her straight away
Y es I love her.

M any happy times together
Y ou and me let's play ball.

D almations are great
O ne and only
G o Flicky.

Evan Byrom (10)
Eastfield Primary School, Hull

Liverpool FC

L iverpool FC
I gnoring our Derby team
V ery concentrated on all the cups
E very fan supporting us
R elentless the team are
P laying games week after week
O n target when scoring goals
O n fire when defending goals
L iving on, even if we're out of cups.

F ootall
C lub.

Ryan Hill (10)
Eastfield Primary School, Hull

The Best

I am the best,
Better than the rest.
I am the strongest,
I am the wealthiest,
I am the best,
I am the best,
I am the hardest,
I am the healthiest.

Ross Carter (11)
Eastfield Primary School, Hull

Tigers

T igers are black and orange. They are very scary.
I gnorant people are hunting them down.
E ndangered they are!
G enerally sleeping. Sniffing for trespassers who are passing by.
E njoy chasing each other and lying down with each other.
R egularly chasing things like birds and butterflies.
S leeping, sighing, wondering what to do next.
Waiting for people to come.

Gemma Hinson (10)
Eastfield Primary School, Hull

Pictures

P ortraits
I n galleries across the world
C overing walls
T ogether in groups
U ntouched through time
R ough paint scraping by fingertips
E ven the paintings seem to
S mile and watch you as you walk.

Laura Baynes (10)
Eastfield Primary School, Hull

Great-Grandma

G reat-Grandma, why did you have to leave?
R ight here with me is where you should be.
A nd everybody misses you, why can't you come back?
N obody can ever replace you in my heart.
D eath is a terrible thing, why choose you?
M y one and only great-grandma
A nyone can see I will miss you till I die.
My great-grandma Johnson.

Erin Anderson (10)
Eastfield Primary School, Hull

Henry

I loved him,
I trusted him,
I will never forget him.
He was my only true friend.
He went away from my life.
I love him and I always will.
Henry.

Olivia Ward (11)
Eastfield Primary School, Hull

Bunnies

B unnies, bunnies all around,
U p they bounce then to the ground
N ever treat them the way you shouldn't
N oses twitching, poops like currants
I t's not hard work you'll soon see
E asy as pie, one, two, three
S mall, cute bunnies.

Ellie Youifon (11)
Eastfield Primary School, Hull

Tigers

T igers are cool, wise animals.
I think they are the greatest animals in the world.
G o to India and you might find one
E veryone thinks tigers are violent animals
R ubbish!
S ome baby tigers are cute.
I love tigers!

Ryan Ian Hakeney (11)
Eastfield Primary School, Hull

Animals

A nimals are becoming endangered
N one of you humans know how upsetting it is
I am an elephant and I am being hunted for my tusks
M ost of my family are already dead
A nd it's all because of you humans
L ots of elephants die every year
S o let's stop killing elephants, right now!

Hannah Louise Waudby (10)
Eastfield Primary School, Hull

Different Animals

A ll animals are different
N ever the same
I think they are all great
M onkeys, tigers, fish,
A nd all the others too
L ike them all, come on!
S top them being extinct, before they're all gone.

Conner William Newman (11)
Eastfield Primary School, Hull

The Sea

T he blue sea reflects the sunlight.
H ear the waves smash on the rocks.
E very night the waves get smaller.

S ometimes you can see the sea shine at night.
E very night you play in the sea with your friends or with me.
A t morning in the sea, the waves come closer to me.

Jack Atkinson (10)
Eastfield Primary School, Hull

Rabbit

R ustling in the bushes
A bout in their cages
B ounding around
B ounding around
I n their gardens.
T he super sunshine is such fun.

Reece Chatfield (10)
Eastfield Primary School, Hull

Mad Dan

There once was a boy called Dan
Who lived in a caravan.
All his friends at school
Thought he was a mad old fool
Because he slept in
An empty swimming pool!

Giselle Redfern (10)
Eastfield Primary School, Hull

I Wish

I wish we could have a world of freedom,
I wish I had everything,
I wish I ruled the world,
I wish I had puppies,
I wish I had lots of chocolate and a chocolate house.
But be sure, this is never going to come true!

Ebru Aktepe (10)
Eastfield Primary School, Hull

Sport

S port is an athletic thing.
P ool is great fun as well
O r playing football
R ather than baseball
T ennis is good and so is basketball.

Matthew Gardner (10)
Eastfield Primary School, Hull

My Little Pony

My little pony
Skinny and bony
Take it to bed
And give it a
Hug.

Sarah Caulfield (11)
Eastfield Primary School, Hull

The Meeting

There once was a boy called Sam,
Who loved eating freshly cooked lamb.
After five days of eating
He went to a meeting
And saw it was a meeting of ham!

Kieran Hornsby (10)
Eastfield Primary School, Hull

Be Me

I don't want to be a . . .
Maker-better,
Child-teacher,
Comet-inspector,
Tooth-taker,
Food-seller,
Creature-carer,
Wood sculptor,
Technology-sorter,
Fish-starer,
Box-talker,
Character-pretender,
Music-maker,
Kingdom-ruler,
Or a . . .
Paper-worker
Paint-splodger,
Seed-planter,
Star-gazer,
Body-bender,
Money-carer,
Thread-sewer,
Dough-dealer,
Book lender,
Liquid-mixer,
Slippery-skater,
Field-plougher,
Hoof-racer.
I want to be me!

Caitlin Stratford (10)
Great Smeaton Primary School, Northallerton

I Like Football

I like to play computer games,
I like to do PE,
I like to ride my bike,
And I like pizza for me tea,
But best of all, I like *football!*

I like to watch The Simpsons on TV.
I like to get pocket money,
I like to work on the farm,
And I like it when it's sunny,
But best of all, I like *football!*

I like to play my euphonium,
I like to go swimming,
I like to get up early,
And I like long distance running,
But best of all, I like *football!*

I like to bounce on the trampoline,
I like the smell of roses,
I like to play with toy cars,
And I like to watch James Bond movies,
But best of all, I like *football!*

Thomas Barley (9)
Great Smeaton Primary School, Northallerton

Animal Poem

Snakes and lakes where hippos live
Crocodiles too
Fish is their favourite food
But watch out you
For owls that say, 'Tu-whit-tu-whoo!'

Try seeing a mouse for dinner
It might be a tight squeeze
But maybe all you will get
Is scrambled cheese.

You should try living with an elephant
It's not that pleasant
You have to clean up its droppings
It's not a very nice job.

Rachel Hinley (8)
Great Smeaton Primary School, Northallerton

Slink Malink

Slink Malink wraps up tight
He hoists up the anchor late at night.
When he wake up he says to himself,
'What a terrible fright,
but now it's light, I'm alright!'

Charlotte Dawes (9)
Great Smeaton Primary School, Northallerton

Is There Room On The Broom?

There was a witch who had a cat, with a very large hat
And long ginger hair which she wore in a plait.
How the cat purred and how the witch grinned
As they sit on their broomstick and flew through the wind.
But how the witch wailed and how the cat spat
When the wind blew wildly the hat suddenly blew off
The witch went down to go and find it
They searched for the hat but it couldn't be found
Then out of the bushes came a thundering dog
With the hat in his jaws
He dropped the hat and said politely,
'Is there room on the broom?'
But the witch wouldn't answer.

Megan Wilson (8)
Great Smeaton Primary School, Northallerton

My Magic Box

(Inspired by 'Magic Box' by Kit Wright)

I will put in my box . . .
The tip of the cheesy moon,
The first hair of a newborn foal rolling in a cosy stable,
The first giggle from a sweet little baby looking up at me!

I will put in my box . . .
The glitter from a shining crystal,
The crack from a see-through iceberg,
The rumbling from an avalanche.

I will put in my box . . .
The familiar smell of a pony's feathery forelock,
A double doughnut with sugary icing,
A shark's tooth.

I will put in my box . . .
A splash of a rolling wave,
A spark from a burning fire.

I will put in my box . . .
My pony and me winning a competition
And a picture of us in the paper.

That's what will go in my box.

Jessica Bassitt (8)
Hampsthwaite Primary School, Hampsthwaite

My Magic Box

(Inspired by 'Magic Box' by Kit Wright)

I will put in my box . . .
The soft silky coat of the cutest kitten,
A dirty ragged footballer in a castle on a throne,
And a beautiful, graceful princess kicking footballs in the finals,
The sharp tip of a shark's ripping tooth.

I will put in my box . . .
A deserted island from far, far away,
A handful of the bluest sky water
In the darkest, scariest cave from Indiana Jones.

I will put in my box . . .
The very last Roman coin that had ever been seen.
A swooping eagle from South Africa on the highest,
dry rock mountain
The biggest chocolate cake in the universe to live on.

I will put in my box . . .
A sharp, powerful palm tree where coconuts as hard as rocks grow
A humongous whale that splashes water at me.

That's what I would put in my box.

Olivia Brown (8)
Hampsthwaite Primary School, Hampsthwaite

Phoenix

Swooping for its prey as aimless as a mole confused in its
own tunnel
Its inferno breath like a scorching wind
More stunning than the Mona Lisa in a British museum
As restoring as the light of God
It's the sun god from the sky
Its crescent beak for sending its soothing bird calls.

Can it really rise from the ashes?

Like people say from the ashes of defeat grow the roses of success
The treacherous depths of its never-ending mind are unreadable
It's the cause of volcanic eruptions
When it soars through the sky, it's as blinding as time travel
It breathes as calm as the Dead Sea coming to the shoreline.

What goes to the sun temple to rest?

When it flies it leaves a trail that looks like the Northern Lights
It's so unique, it doesn't breed
Searching for human life form
It's so thoughtful and yet cold-blooded
Its eyesight as sharp as a piece of carved ice.

Will Dawson (8)
Hampsthwaite Primary School, Hampsthwaite

The Phoenix

The phoenix - as fiery as a huge, amazing sun
That shines upon me.

As shiny as a golden, bright star
Glowing in the dark.

As mythical as a rising dragon
That has a fiery inferno breath.

Burning like a mythical lion that could rise from the sun
And could swoop through millions of fire flames.

As light as a blazing bright light
With eyes like a sharp pointy dagger
That can burn you up just by looking at them.

Who has golden wings?
Who has inferno breath?
Who has eyes like daggers?
Who has fire on its tail?
Who has a soul as hard as a brick?

Its name is revealed as the *phoenix!*

Tom Payne (8)
Hampsthwaite Primary School, Hampsthwaite

The Phoenix

As golden as a light feather.
As hot as a dark sun.
As sunny as a purple sun.

As sandy as a yellow Egypt.
As bright as a burning, rising sun.
As powerful as a red, hot dragon.

Fire is like a multicoloured umbrella.
Burning like flaming winter sprites.
Music is like a phoenix rising from the hot ground.

The fire is like a rocket on fire.
It is like a giant flying through the air.
Burning as a French seal in water that is hot as ashes.

His tears are like hailstones dropping on heavy water.
The wings are powerful but the feathers reflect on the water.
The colours are strong and he flies like lightning.

The phoenix!

Kimberley Beecroft (7)
Hampsthwaite Primary School, Hampsthwaite

My Magic Box

(Inspired by 'Magic Box' by Kit Wright)

I will put in my box . . .
The super, soothing neigh of a silvery pony
And a gorgeous, gleaming, lovely lilac amethyst.
A great smell of star fizz.

I will put in my box . . .
Divine acornade from the golden tree
And a unicorn's tail swishing in the cool breeze.
A luxurious pinch of a koala's fur.

My box is made of sparkling moonbeams
And silver stars which make it bright gold.

I will travel to Fairyland and dance all night
Under the shining stars, guiding my way
To the crowded dance floor.

That's why it's my magic box!

Emma Milnes (8)
Hampsthwaite Primary School, Hampsthwaite

My Magic Box

(Inspired by 'Magic Box' by Kit Wright)

I will put in my box . . .
The biggest chocolate bar
A pet dog to play with forever
I would hear the sound of laughter.

I will put in my box . . .
Lavender with the sweetest smell
Fluffy sheep leaping over mountain rocks
A photograph of my brown and white puppy chasing her tail.

I will put in my box . . .
A family photo to keep the memories special
The best thing in the world.

My box is sparkly with strips
And a secret agent bodyguard watch hole!

Alex Wylie (7)
Hampsthwaite Primary School, Hampsthwaite

Friendship

A little feeling from inside
Which is made to create friendship,
From a boy to girl or girl to girl,
It still will mean a rising.

Many people who share a friendship
Have a little falling out,
But if falling out or not,
Don't let that bring you apart.

Many people who like each other
Are forgiving, helpful and admiring,
But don't let jealousy strike you
Or your friendship will fall apart.

Lucie Algret (9)
Hampsthwaite Primary School, Hampsthwaite

The Phoenix

He has wings longer than you can imagine
Feathers as long as ten buses
What is he?

Golden body burning with flames of anger
A beak as smooth as new woven silk
What is he?

Eyes eager to find his prey and catch it
Extinct from existence
What is he?

This mysterious bird is the . . .
Phoenix!

Lewis Cameron (9)
Hampsthwaite Primary School, Hampsthwaite

My Magic Box

(Inspired by 'Magic Box' by Kit Wright)

I will put in my box . . .
Galloping horses across the meadows.

I will put in my box . . .
The first baby's smile
The first puppy's bark
The first purr of a kitten.

I will put in my box . . .
A lovely lollipop to lick on a boiling, burning day
The feel of warm air blowing into my face.
The smell of orange juice.

Elizabeth Weatherill (8)

Hampsthwaite Primary School, Hampsthwaite

My Walk In The Wood

I see eerie, old, deceptive trees
Leaning in to where I stand,
Their branches spread like fingers
From a gnarled hand.
Leaves flutter silently around my head,
Others fall in swirling patterns
Until they reach their dirty bed.
Dry twigs crack beneath my hesitant feet,
As I look up the trees no longer meet.
I stumble out of the wood and feel a chilly breeze,
The last thing I see is rough bark bringing
Character to the trees . . .

Zoë Anderson (11)

Kirkby & Great Broughton Primary School, Stokesley

Hailstones

As hailstones fall I suddenly stare,
It's just like an animal returning to a lair.
Drip,
Slip,
Drop down, down, down,
Hailstones crying out loud,
Falling,
    Dripping,
        To the
            Ground.

As I hear them I think
What if I were one of them?
So I watch as they cover the grass and stems.
They are like
    Bullets,
        But as
            Light
                As feathers.

Suddenly they stop,
Everything as still as a statue.
I hear someone coming, but who?
I go
    Inside
        And hide.

Amber Madden (10)
Kirkby & Great Broughton Primary School, Stokesley

Weather

Twisting,
Turning,
Spinning,

Charging through the town
I'm a natural bomb.
Up and down, up and down,
With the force of a mad storm.

Nothing is left behind,
Only shattered dreams
And memories . . .

Racing, never stopping;
As thoughtless as a drunk,
Rising and dropping, rising and dropping,
Landing with a thump.

Swivelling,
Revolving,
Rotating,

Nothing is left behind,
Only shattered dreams
And memories . . .

I'm a hurricane.

Molly Worth (11)
Kirkby & Great Broughton Primary School, Stokesley

Treacle People

In a magical place
Where blipple blops are,
There's some tiny people
Who come from afar.

They eat nothing but treacle,
It rains from the sky,
So they all have buckets
Which they hold up high.

Once they are done
They run straight home
To a pink and blue mansion
In the shape of a dome.

They climb down a tunnel,
Incredibly deep,
And when they are tired
They fall straight to sleep.

This was the story of the treacle clan
Who love the sugary goo,
And if you saw them in the street
I ask, what would you do?

Lili Wake (10)
Kirkby & Great Broughton Primary School, Stokesley

The Trapped Lion

I once saw a trapped lion
In a zoo one day in May,
Where little children tapped the glass
Then continued on their way.

The lion looked so very sad
And pleaded with his large brown eyes
For freedom and to leave the zoo,
And his cage that was a tiny size.

The keeper let the poor beast out
Before tying him with a chain,
Which led to a collar as tight as a knot
And cut into his hay-like mane.

The great, ragged lion was forced to do tricks
As the cruel crowd smiled and laughed.
I felt annoyed and angry as a shark
While everyone giggled as if they were daft.

When the lion was at last put back in his cage
He was clearly hurt and full of pain,
So I made up my mind right then and decided
Never to visit a zoo again.

Laura Smith (10)

Kirkby & Great Broughton Primary School, Stokesley

Winner

The Mysterious Wood

I knew it would be a strange night,
But my senses led me outside.
I turned the corner, towards the wood,
The wind whistling in my ear like a howling wolf.
I could see many little lights,
But still I couldn't see.
I walked straight into the dingy wood
As if I was hypnotised.

I saw huge old oak trees standing crooked,
Their branches spread widely.
Their shadows: witches' fingers,
Rough bark with big, strange holes.
Two red dots lingered inside:
A flashlight in the dark.
Leaves fluttered rapidly
As if someone was shaking its branch.
Some leaves fell;
Firstly curving slightly,
Then elegantly touching the ground.
Twigs cracked under my feet,
Breaking the deadly silence.

Kate Seymour (11)
Kirkby & Great Broughton Primary School, Stokesley

I'm A Mess

I am very messy as you can see,
The scruffiest person must be me.

Some people call me a disgrace
Whenever I fall over my shoelace.

My brother is a tidy boy,
With a clean room, full of joy.

I have tomato ketchup in my bed,
And a teddy bear with no head.

My toys are scattered all over the floor
And I have spiders on my bedroom door.

I have yoghurt stains all over my dress,
But tidying my room is not a success.

When I eat I have my arms on the table,
I only do this because it makes my head stable.

So I'm the most messiest person you might know,
This isn't the last you have seen of me, not yet, *no!*

Jessica Ivin (8)
Kirkby & Great Broughton Primary School, Stokesley

The Fruit Bowl

Grapes are small, green and round,
Like a little smiley face with his friends.
Apples are fat and yummy,
Red as a rose and shiny and ripe.
Pineapples are green and orange.

Rosa Lusvardi (9)
Kirkby & Great Broughton Primary School, Stokesley

Cold Days In Winter

C oats are put on
O ld stormy wind swoops over land
L ights shine over the clear white snow
D ays go by much quicker

D ogs and children play in the snow
A nimals whimper in the cold
'Y eah!' children cry when snow falls
S un hides behind the world

I gloos are made by children
N eat gardens droop and die

W ild and vicious storms come
I nsects hide under the ground
N aughty children throw snowballs
T eachers close schools
E ven children think it is too cold to play
R ain falls in heavy showers.

Polly Day (9)
Kirkby & Great Broughton Primary School, Stokesley

The Rabbit

It was a dark, dingy night,
There was nothing in sight,
Not even a sound,
Apart from the rabbit hopping around.

The rabbit was completely clueless
That it would soon be a total mess,
Because it would be run over
By a car or a Land Rover.

It could not see the road at all
Because the road was big and it was small.
It scampered across without a care,
Soon it would get an awful scare.

A car sped past without braking,
Though he could see the rabbit shaking,
And due to his cruelty the rabbit died,
If he'd just braked, it would have survived.

Laura Jackson (11)
Kirkby & Great Broughton Primary School, Stokesley

The Twists Of Life

All life is, is a long corridor
With so many paths to choose.
Every day a new door opens,
You thinking of the way.
One door is love and one hate,
Another your job and one your greed.
One good and one bad,
And when you choose you'd love to turn back.
And every day you wonder
What tomorrow will bring.
All your life you travel,
Looking for a day when
You will find your way,
And you often wonder,
Lord, when will be my day?

Nick Brown (11)
Kirkby & Great Broughton Primary School, Stokesley

Down In The Basement

Down in the basement there is:
A photo of Simon Cowell,
An old sewing machine,
A picture of an Olympic runner from Beijing,
One old, smelly sock,
Some medicine from chickenpox
And a model of a super marine Spitfire.
There's something in the basement
And it's me!

Luke Taylor (10)
Kirkby & Great Broughton Primary School, Stokesley

Our School

At our school we have salad for food
And you will not be rude.

We wear red uniform for school
And our teacher is extremely cool!

We have assembly at half-past ten,
And we can write in pen.

Some afternoons we have art
And it looks extremely smart.

Some days we have physical education
And history around the nation.

So our school is fun every day,
And we've been to Robin Hood's Bay.

Samuel Donaldson (10)
Kirkby & Great Broughton Primary School, Stokesley

Twisted Trees

Twisted trees which look like monsters,
Branches spread out like witches' fingers,
Leaves flutter like a bird flying in the wind,
Leaves fall like swirling snowflakes.

Twigs crack under my feet like a
Ruler just been snapped.
I see rough bark like
Dead skin on your feet.

Chloe Coverdale (11)
Kirkby & Great Broughton Primary School, Stokesley

A Park In Winter

In a park in winter
It's as silent as a mouse,
Just like a Christmas story tale
Ready to be read out.

The snow goes down like drumbeats,
As fast as Santa's sleigh,
I hear the howling wind
Looking for somewhere to stay.

I smell the burning fire,
Just like on Christmas Day.
The smell of cold makes my nose ring,
As a school bell about to ding.

Charlotte Smith (10)
Kirkby & Great Broughton Primary School, Stokesley

The Circus

I like the circus,
I watch it roll into town.
I hear the animals calling,
But I wait for the clowns.
The trapeze on high,
The acrobats jump and twirl.
I see the ringmaster's hat.
The elephants do a jig,
The tent is so big.
We'll come back again
When the circus is back in town!

Aimée Anderson (8)
Kirkby & Great Broughton Primary School, Stokesley

Spring Wakes Up

Drip, drip, drop, the snow has to go.
The snowman's nose has fallen, oh no!
All the snow melts from the ground,
Now the air feels like spring is around.

New animals start to be born,
The fields start to grow corn.
Lots of animals begin to come out
Then the trees start to sprout.

The morning birds start their singing,
Then the ducklings will start swimming.
Then the children return to school,
After that you can swim in the pool.

Francesca Ablett (8)
Kirkby & Great Broughton Primary School, Stokesley

One Summer's Day!

The sun is bright,
The day is right
And it is such a beautiful sight.

The blue sky is clear
And sweet birds you hear,
And in the forest there is a beautiful grazing deer.

The sweet smell of flowers,
Which wafts in your face
As soon as you pass,
What a lovely summer's day!

Lorna Harrison (9)
Kirkby & Great Broughton Primary School, Stokesley

The Bird

He flies high and low,
In and out of the spiny trees.
The flying insects have no chance
Against the fast flying bird.

He flies high and low
Collecting insects for his nest.
Tiny chicks chirp happily
When a fly comes their way.

He flies high and low,
Enjoying the evening air,
And when the sun sets,
He settles down for a long night's sleep.

Samuel Day (11)
Kirkby & Great Broughton Primary School, Stokesley

Naughty, Naughty

'You're a silly boy, Peter.'
'No I am not.'
'You're a liar, liar, your bum's on fire
And you're halfway up the telephone wire,
And your bum's a real big tyre.'
'Ahhhh!'
'Ha, ha.'

Georgia Irving (8)
Kirkby & Great Broughton Primary School, Stokesley

The City In The Kitchen

Crash, bang, wallop.
Down comes the butter
Down comes the sugar
And down come the people.
Up the pole and down the pole,
Collect and take,
Mix and stir,
A hundred people all at once.
Cook and fry,
Flip and catch,
And in half a minute,
Eat.

Isabelle Day (8)
Kirkby & Great Broughton Primary School, Stokesley

Robotic Grandad

So robotic, can't even move,
Sat down all day, he needs a snooze,
Poke him and prod him and make him turn on.

Knows all the facts from long ago,
And might need a stick to help him along,
Ask him a question, he'll search it all through.

He'll find the answer, I just know he will!
But it's disappointing when he stops still.
Wiggle him and jiggle him and make him awake.

Time for a nap now he's been on all day!

Lucy Husband (10)
Kirk Hammerton CE Primary School, York

Ice, Snow And Wind

The ice is a white tiger
Sliding
When dinner comes
There's mess everywhere
He is a killer cat
Hunting.

The snow is like a white horse
Galloping from the sky
Carefully camouflaged
Searching for somewhere to hide.

The wind is a wolf
Howling on rooftops
What a racket
She has woken me up.

Emma Ward (9)
Kirk Hammerton CE Primary School, York

Big Uncle Albert!

Soft and mushy
like Mum's beans.
Hard on the outside,
soft in the middle.
Big uncle Albert
his big round belly,
just like a beanbag.
Snuggle up, snuggle up,
don't let him go!

Emma Lock (10)
Kirk Hammerton CE Primary School, York

Boring Brother

He's a vast desert,
My brother,
Wide and plain,
Nothing for miles,
A blank mind.

No expression
Or character,
Or fun.

He never says sentences,
But words out of the blue.
Like a sandstorm,
So still, so quiet, but then -
A burst of life!

Cora Herbert (10)
Kirk Hammerton CE Primary School, York

Glass Snowman

When I went to Planet Tass
I saw a snowman made of glass.
He said, 'Hello' and suddenly then
He just became a fountain pen.

Then I got into my car
A turbo ZZ Belisaar.
I fell off the edge of the cliff
Twelve thousand feet to Planet Miff.

Tom Hooper (10)
Kirk Hammerton CE Primary School, York

The Scary Fog

The fog is like a burglar
Coming out at night.
You'd better watch out
Because he will give you a fright.

Oliver Robertshaw (10)
Kirk Hammerton CE Primary School, York

Book

I flick through my life
Turning pages as I go
Seeing happy things
Growing old and happy.

Stewart Keddie (10)
Kirk Hammerton CE Primary School, York

What Am I?

Floppy cheeks,
Colossal paws,
Stumped tail,
Wrinkly skin,
Huge eyes,
And a bottom sniffer.
What am I?

James Carr (10)
Le Cateau Community Primary School, Catterick Garrison

Angry Dad And The Family

My dad puts his pants on with a struggle,
Flanders next door gives his children a snuggle,
But my mom is the one who gets the blame,
She should be up the nagging hall of fame.
Mr Burns is cheap, he has a lackey called Smithers,
He is so crooked, he even slithers.
Chief Wiggam is a lazy officer dude,
He even goes in the streets being ever so rude.
My dad got a mace and said, 'I'll mace you up for good.'
I shouted, *'Argh,'* but he never understood.
Krusty the clown, my old legend hero,
Turned out today he was officially zero.
I went to Milhouse when he was kissing a girl called Marumba,
As a classic I shouted, 'Ay carumba!'
Seymour Skinner, my old, stupid principal
Said that I wasn't as good as sensible Willie,
The Scottish, red-bearded lackey.
He really sounds just like a Jackie.
Lisa the dork, my sister, smells like feet,
It's really funny, she doesn't eat meat.
Fat Tony, the gang mob boss,
He really is the one who they call Hoss.
Professor Frink, he's mean, is a weirdo,
He is just like my teacher, Mr Meido.
Maggie, the one who shot Mr Burns,
She hates the kid called Toby Murns.
I am Bart, the really cool, hey
I show my butt to the class every day.
I am more cool than a wind-blowing fan.
This is Bart Simpson, don't stay in school, man.

Aaron Nunn (10)
Le Cateau Community Primary School, Catterick Garrison

Guess What He Is

He's black,
He's white,
He's cute,
He's cuddly,
He's aggressive,
He scratches,
He bites,
He's lazy,
He's skinny,
He's small,
He pounces,
He's quick,
He's puffy,
He's soft,
He's jolly,
He's fast,
He hates to stay,
Loves to eat,
Loves to play,
Hates to wait.

Stacey Whelan (11)
Le Cateau Community Primary School, Catterick Garrison

Rattlesnakes

R attle in the day and night
A nd they can see in the dark
T he deadly fangs
T errifying their prey
L ive in Mexico
E at a whole rat in one
S leep curled up in a coil
N ever disturb rattlesnakes
A rattlesnake can sense movement
K ills rats with its poison
E ggs hatch into a small snake
S leeps in a hole.

Lewis Shevlin (10)
Le Cateau Community Primary School, Catterick Garrison

Easter

Easter's the best time for me,
Everything goes right, you see.
Chocolate eggs and much, much more,
Nothing ever is a bore.
Family, friends and everyone,
There will be even more fun!

All the kids are looking for the Easter bunny,
Actually, really it is quite funny.
Baby lambs, calves and sheep,
Soon all will be fast asleep!

Hannah Burston (10)
Le Cateau Community Primary School, Catterick Garrison

About Valentine's Day

V alentine's Day is about love
A ll you love is your valentine
L est there be left a present
E verything is only a valentine and love
N ever dump a valentine
T ime for the love god to come
I nside the heart is love
N ever forget a gift
E ver you don't forget the day
S o you have everything.

Ben Barker (9)
Le Cateau Community Primary School, Catterick Garrison

The Blitz

City destroyers,
Evacuation makers,
People killers,
Noise makers,
Life riskers,
Fire creators,
Night attackers,
Home wreckers,
Bomb droppers.

Robert McKay (9)
Le Cateau Community Primary School, Catterick Garrison

I Am A . . .

I can eat people,
I can fly up high in the sky,
I am aggressive towards my owners,
I am big when I am on land,
Also small when I'm in the sky,
I cannot be cute and cuddly,
I have sharp claws and teeth,
I hate to stay still.
Do you know what I am?

Natasha Kinloch (9)
Le Cateau Community Primary School, Catterick Garrison

A Boxer

There is a man called Rocky Balboa,
He is a boxer, he is the best.
He has beaten everyone,
In the championship and the rest.
Rocky has beaten Mr T and Thunderlips,
And especially the big cheat from Russia!
Rocky's name in boxing is the Italian Stallion.
His real name is Sylvester Stallone.
I also like Rambo.

Ewan Upton (10)
Le Cateau Community Primary School, Catterick Garrison

It's A Riddle!

It gets into your house and steals your food,
It wears a rope around its neck.
It digs and rolls in mud,
Has big ears and a long fluffy tail.
It gives nasty bites with its razor-sharp teeth,
It can take you down, but can be nice.
If you are nice it will love you.
It makes a lot of noise and loves to play.
What is it?

Ethan Blanchard (9)
Le Cateau Community Primary School, Catterick Garrison

The Blitz

Planes flying,
People dying,
Bombs exploding,
Guns loading,
Bullets hitting,
Tanks fitting,
Grenades booming,
Sirens *whooming.*
This is World War II!

Thomas Featherstone (9)
Le Cateau Community Primary School, Catterick Garrison

Explorer

E xplore the cave for gems
X -ray vision to see traps
P iles of dirty old bones
L oads of coffins with skeletons inside
O r there could be gold and treasures
R ampage of rats across the floor
E xplorers look for stuff and more
R olling coins, rattling chains, the
explorer said, 'Let's do it again!'

Ross McCallum (9)
Le Cateau Community Primary School, Catterick Garrison

The Devil

T he Devil is scary!
H orns as big as elephant trunks
E vil as a dragon

D evils live in Hell
E xchange lives for souls
V ertical horns as sharp as a knife
I ntelligent as a chicken
L azy as a cow.

Ben Edwards (10)
Le Cateau Community Primary School, Catterick Garrison

Am I Light Or Am I Bright?

The stars are bright,
The stars are blue,
The stars are red
And they follow you.

Moon, moon, light and bright,
You shine this very night.
Sky, sky, you are pale blue.
Sunshine, sunshine, I follow you.

Mirren Worsdale (10)
Le Cateau Community Primary School, Catterick Garrison

Animals

Animals are scary,
Some are hair.
Some birds can't fly,
Some birds can die.
Animals have fights,
They are never polite.
The bear is walking,
Animals aren't talking.

Anmol Procha Rai (11)
Le Cateau Community Primary School, Catterick Garrison

The One You Love

People express their love on this day
Just so you know, it's not in May.
They bake cakes and sell them on,
They're yummy and scrummy.
Though it's not sunny
Tell the one you love
That you love them,
You won't regret it.

Lucy O'Flanagan (9)
Le Cateau Community Primary School, Catterick Garrison

The Blitz

When I joined the army
I went in a fight.
It went on
All through the night.
I got shot by a bullet,
But there ain't no damage,
In the mornin',
My leg's in a bandage.

John Gilbert (10)
Le Cateau Community Primary School, Catterick Garrison

Pancakes

P int of milk
A bit of flour
N ot too much lemon
C hocolate as well, if you like chocolate
A pinch of sugar to make it sweet
K eep the pancake warm
E at as much as you can
S ee it disappear.

Aaron Johnson-Taylor (10)
Le Cateau Community Primary School, Catterick Garrison

The Explorer

Plants falling,
Machetes swinging,
Flies buzzing,
Mosquitoes biting,
Leopards growling,
Lions roaring,
Birds chirping,
Animals eating.

Joshua Baines (10)
Le Cateau Community Primary School, Catterick Garrison

Seashore

S eashore, seashore the waves going out of control
E ating sandwiches, covered with sand
A mongst the waves look at the dolphins swimming
S wimming in the sea
H ot, so hot on the seashore
O n the seabed fishes swimming along
R ound and round you run on the beach
E ither hot or cold, I go there every day.

Narita Limbu (10)
Le Cateau Community Primary School, Catterick Garrison

Love Machine

I am a lean, mean love machine,
I'll say it three times, so stay back or say goodbye.
I am a lean, mean love machine,
Stay back, I'll say it again,
Stay back or say goodbye.
So am I right or am I wrong?
Because I am a lean, mean love machine.

Michael Ellis (9)
Le Cateau Community Primary School, Catterick Garrison

Unicorns

U nicorns fly high in the sky
N ight comes, we are alive
I n the darkness we glow
C olours of the rainbow
O n my pure white head I have a single horn
R unning through the forest
N ever to be seen!

Chloe Middleton (10)
Le Cateau Community Primary School, Catterick Garrison

Jungle

The jungle is cold,
The jungle is wet,
The jungle is funny, I bet!
Sometimes it's hot
And sometimes it's cold,
Sometimes it's wet
And sometimes it's not.

Mellissa Williams (10)
Le Cateau Community Primary School, Catterick Garrison

Dragons

D angerous
R ough
A ggressive
G reen as grass
O ptimistic
N asty
S cary.

William Johnston (10)
Le Cateau Community Primary School, Catterick Garrison

The Cool Fish!

His name is Goggles,
His mind always boggles.
Whenever you touch him he will bite
And sometimes he acts like a little sprite.
Then he always poses,
Finally the bowl closes!

Ty McIvor (10)
Le Cateau Community Primary School, Catterick Garrison

Guess What?

Meat-eater,
Water swimmer,
Swamp liver,
Cold-blooded,
Camouflaged green,
Beady eyes.

Kyle Frew-McGill (10)
Le Cateau Community Primary School, Catterick Garrison

Tigers!

T erribly scary
I ntrepid hunters
G reedy eaters
E motional
R oary is his name
S harp teeth.

Rebecca Willetts (10)
Le Cateau Community Primary School, Catterick Garrison

What Am I?

Venom spitter,
Teeth, sharp as razor blades,
Fast as lightning,
Killer machine,
It hates everything,
It can eat everything it can find.

Dean Stephen Watson (9)
Le Cateau Community Primary School, Catterick Garrison

The Blanket Of Fog

He pulls his mysterious grey cloak over the city.
Slowly, one by one, the streets turn grey,
Until very inch of the city is covered by him.
He cackles with glee.
He floats above the city, motionless.
He is an evil, thick cloud of small droplets
Of poisonous water that sting you if you touch them.
But he is alone; a lonely fool.
He sweeps through the streets
Spreading his strange steam all over them,
Like butter spreading on toast.
He leaves fear behind him, a bad feeling
That will never desert you.
He sets off towards the remaining ruins,
Guilt etched on every corner of his face.
He damages the cities so badly that
They lose all their pleasure and value.
He is the blanket of fog.

Gulce Ozkan (10)
Lord Deramore's Primary School, York

The Sea

The glittering sea shining under the sun's smiling beams,
Children squeal running in and out on the shore.

But the sea is best in the night.

Under the stars' watchful eyes,
I sit on the pier and cry.
The sea is so beautiful
When the gentle waves break.
I look out towards the horizon.

The sea is best in the night.

The sea is sleeping, dreaming,
But still travelling far.
The waves, that tonight stop here,
On the other side of the world tomorrow,
Like a magical, never-ending sleepwalk.

The sea is best in the night.

When the sea whispers to me,
It tells me to come closer.
I long to follow its journey
Across to foreign lands,
But I know I must stay here to guard the sea.

The sea needs me in the night.

During the storms the sea cannot sleep,
However during the calm nights
The sea is a good listener.
It splashes in sympathy or agreement.

I need the sea in the night.

The sea needs me, I need the sea,
And it is truly, truly best in the night.

Catriona Thornton (11)
Lord Deramore's Primary School, York

Anger

I am waiting,
Waiting in the breeze.

I am waiting for the anger
Deep inside me to wake.

Finally I find it,
With it raging deep down.
I tower into the air.

I stretch down my arms
Grabbing everything,
Everything in sight.

Crunching and eating my victims,
Then with my swirling body
I slam them to the ground.

As I sweep along the city,
The rubble is my snail trail.

But when the anger dies down
I grow weaker
And I get sucked back into the darkness.

I am the twister, the mighty twister!

Hannah Conibere (11)
Lord Deramore's Primary School, York

The Day After

The night before had been rowdy.
The wind huffed and puffed down heavy,
Like a bag of stones on the Earth.

This was the day after.

The atmosphere swirled a whirlpool of gloom,
Turning the sky from blue to grey.
The moon stole secretly away and slunk out of sight,
Ready to rest until darkness overtook once again.

This was the day after.

Shyly, the stars hid their brilliance behind a misty mask,
Eventually disappearing, only to return when
Their slumber was disturbed by the storm crashing by,
Waking all the weather with a vengeance.

Headachy thunder crashed whilst tiny, yet
Bullet-like, sharp hailstones attacked,
Making the furious thunder rumble and grumble louder.
The Earth shook, disturbed by the noise.

This was the day after.

Ella Batters (10)
Lord Deramore's Primary School, York

The Composer

If I was ever to be in danger,
In danger of leaving for good,
What would you do?
What would you say?
Would you let me leave you?
Would you let me stay,
Fight side by side
Till the very end?
If your answer is yes,
I need you now!
The music inside me leaves me.
Changing from black to white
And back.
Winter, spring, summer and autumn
Merge into one.
I have left.
I am saved.
I need a composer,
Compose me again.
The music is gone, play me more.

Kathryn Bruce (11)
Lord Deramore's Primary School, York

The White Horse

The white horse forms way out to sea.
It comes charging the cliffs,
Foam-steam coming out of its nostrils.

It reaches the beach,
Its eyes searching madly
For something unseen.

It is a warning
For those who can read it,
But no one can.

It hits the cliff,
Nothing can stop it.
The last warning has gone.

It splits into many parts,
They trickle back to the sea.
Out to sea forms a typhoon.

Hugh Gammon (11)
Lord Deramore's Primary School, York

The Water Musician

The whispers from the sea were soft
As it came closer to the sleeping land.
The waves made a calm sound
That made the whole of creation
Join in with the sweet melody.
This is the water musician.

Hanjun Kim (11)
Lord Deramore's Primary School, York

What Is . . . The Snow?

The snow is a white cover.
Snow has come and is really beautiful.

Walk on the snow
We can hear some sound,
It is really funny.

We can play with snow, how?
Play snow fights or make snowmen,
And we can go skiing.

The lake changes to ice,
You check and if it is right,
You can go on the ice
But it is really dangerous,
And I said, 'Don't go on,'
Because we don't know
When the ice is broken.

Hong Yoon (10)
Lord Deramore's Primary School, York

The Oak Tree

The oak tree is the keeper of the forest, guarding the woods.
It is the king of all plants, reaching to the sun.
It is a wooden giant, never falling down.
It is a man with many arms, his fingers reaching up to the clouds.
It is an immoveable object, watching all the others.

Joshua Gray (11)
Lord Deramore's Primary School, York

Silence

Once there was silence in the valley;
We could hear the slow whisper of the trees,
The calm thoughts of the mountains,
The soft breeze of the clouds.
Then came the people
Chopping trees,
Not hearing the screams,
Not hearing the pain.
The slow whisper of the trees became a cry,
The calm thought of the mountains became nightmares.
Once there was silence,
Now there is pain.

Louise Oliver (11)
Lord Deramore's Primary School, York

The Sun

The sun is a golden sphere
Dropped in a muddy puddle.

It is a golden plate
Left on the table of the universe.

It is a torch
Shining through the fabric of the universe.

It is an eye of the gods
Staring pitifully on Earth.

The sun is a firework
Frozen in time.

Hamish Campbell-Smith (10)
Lord Deramore's Primary School, York

Half World

She changes shape,
She is a mirror;
Giving us light that is not hers.
She is a mirror;
A mirror of life,
She gives us light,
Light in the night.
She is always around
Yet she hides it,
Like we hide our mood.
She is lunar, the moon.

George Hitchon Godfrey (10)
Lord Deramore's Primary School, York

The Blanket Of Fog

The gloomy stare showed it all,
The patience about to pay off.
As the black velvet sky drew to a peak,
The fog descended on to its prey
Like a lion clinging to a helpless antelope
On the brim of death.
But this time it was the houses in trouble,
Hopeless and stranded with no movement,
Hoping for the best.
But the best will not come
As the fog has already descended.

Harry Collins (11)
Lord Deramore's Primary School, York

The Sun

The sun is the breath of a dragon
Drowning in a sea of blue.
Tireless; it shines,
Never stopping, never failing.
It is a smiling face
Shining down on our planet.
It is a golden rock pool
Full of life.
It is life really,
At its heart . . .

Joseph Copland (11)
Lord Deramore's Primary School, York

A Green Wonderland

I am a green wonderland,
A monkey's maze,
A land of silk,
A million different colours,
A singing breeze.
I am as tall, as tall as can be,
I sing myself to sleep at night.
Prowling predators lurking here and there,
Dark and deadly,
Powerful but strong.

Surya Sanderson (10)
Lord Deramore's Primary School, York

Always Try Your Best

If I lived in the deep blue sky,
I'd sleep upon the clouds of fluff,
Listen to the gentle lullaby
And show the world how much I love.

If I could change the nature's kind
All over this dying land we call home,
The horrid memories would be left behind
And would be a fading thought in a fossil stone.

If I had only one day to live the experience,
I would create as much as I could to help others.
I'd travel from London to Spain, to France,
And meet my friends, sisters and brothers.

If I could change the rules and laws,
They would be to help citizens to live.
They would be hung up on every door,
So people could understand and give.

If I could be a royal princess,
My friends would all get gifts to treasure.
I'd buy myself a diamond dress
And give myself and friends lots of leisure.

This world is full of possibilities,
So try the best you can,
Across all the oceans and all the seas,
Because one day you could own the land.

Rebecca Brown (11)

Markington CE Primary School, Harrogate

What I Wanna Do . . .

I wanna be an admired designer
Of family buildings and beautiful houses.
People will look at them
And say, 'Oh, wow,
This building is great.
Great, great, great.'
I wanna see the northern lights,
Bright, bright green
Like the summer grass.
They would hang like
Curtains from the sky.
Snap, snap, snap,
My camera would say.
I wanna be a famous author
Writing books in my secret study.
Books of magic, books of mystery,
I would write them both.
People want to
Read, read, read.
I wanna design amazing clothes,
Spring, summer, autumn or winter,
I would design cool clothes for all.
Everyone would
Boogie, woogie, woogie.

Vicky Frost (10)
Markington CE Primary School, Harrogate

The Luckiest Girl In The World!

If I lived forever I would see how tall the oak tree grows.
If I had a tail I could swim through the ocean
And look at the beautiful fish gliding with their colourful scales.
If I was as tall as a mountain I could touch the dazzling stars
Glittering in the sky with pride.
If I had a shell I could hear the whales humming beneath the waves.
If I glowed as bright as a lamp I would shine wherever it is dark.
If I had a magic carpet I would fly high in the sky
And touch the soft cotton clouds.
If I could hear through walls I would listen to the things
I can, but not the things I can't.
If I had a lucky charm I would keep it as long as I want
But pass it on to someone who needs it more.
If I was as small as a butterfly I would
Show off my beauty with pride and dignity.
If I had an airplane I would fly to the top of the tallest mountain
And look at the world below me.
If I walked to the end of the rainbow I would not keep
The pot of gold to myself, I would share it with the person
Who followed in my footsteps and believed
It was not impossible to do.
If I could have and do all these things,
I would be the luckiest girl in the world!

Sophie Reed (11)
Markington CE Primary School, Harrogate

The Lonely Poem

'I want peace all over the world,'
Echoed the sky.
'I want to stop fighting,'
Said the soldier.
'I want to help people,'
Echoed Jesus.
'I don't want to go off,'
Boomed the bomb.
'I don't want to erupt,'
Cackled the volcano.
'I want to live,'
Cracked the tree.
'I want to be fed,'
Rumbled the hungry tummy.
'I don't want to die,'
Said the old lady.
'I want to help people,'
Boomed the sky.
'I don't want to make things worse,'
Cried the bullet.

Catherine Stamp (11)
Markington CE Primary School, Harrogate

Lost Souls

'I want to go home,'
Trembled the lost life.
'I want my child back,'
Roared Mother Earth.
'I want to be played with,'
Squeaked the lost toy.
'I want to save someone's life,'
Boomed the loving bullet.
'I don't want to leave my family,'
Trembled the terrified soul.
'I don't want to destroy,'
Boomed the bomb.
'I don't want to spread,'
Gurgled the sickness.
'I don't want to kill,'
Boomed the missile.
'I need to write,'
Scribbled the pencil.
'I need to shine,'
Choked the light bulb.

Lachlan Nicholson (10)
Markington CE Primary School, Harrogate

Please Change

'I want to look over the land,'
Rustled the huge tree.
'I want to gallop freely,'
Roared the king of the jungle.
'I want to jump and flip,'
Squeaked the dolphin.
'I want to look after land and sea,'
Groaned the world.
'I want to build nests in the trees,'
Chirped the sparrow.
'I want to go home,'
Screamed the experimental chimpanzee.
'I want the world back to what it was,'
Moaned Mother Nature.

Helen Jennings (10)
Markington CE Primary School, Harrogate

I Have A Dream

'I don't want to harm anybody,'
Boomed the dangerous bullet.
'I want to be jammed,'
Clicked the machine gun.
'I don't want to be blown up,'
Rattled the ground.
'I want to be defused,'
Roared the missile.
'I don't want to be annihilated,'
Cried the dying soldier.

Joshua Macey (9)
Markington CE Primary School, Harrogate

I Want!

'I don't want to chop,'
Said the axe.
'I don't want to burn,'
Roared the fire.
'We don't want to die,'
Mimed the trees.
'I wish I could stay,'
Whispered the old man.
'I don't want to kill,'
Cried the bullet.
'I don't want to destroy,'
Boomed the bomb.
'I don't want to die,'
Sobbed the injured soldier.

Samuel Hubbard (9)
Markington CE Primary School, Harrogate

Space

Moon maker,
Star striker,
Planet passer,
Comet creator,
Rocket racer,
Shuttle scraper,
Sky seer,
Alien amuser,
Satellite sender.

Matty Jones (8)
Markington CE Primary School, Harrogate

I Have A Dream . . .

'I want to live,'
Cried the hunted crocodile,
'But how do I?'
'I want to dodge hopeless people,'
Boomed the bullet.
'I want to survive,'
Sobbed the whale.
'I don't want to go to Heaven,'
Cried the old man in pain and in horror.
'I don't want to leave my family,'
Sobbed the young soldier.
'I don't want to leave Planet Earth,'
Bellowed everything in fury.

Robbie Wilberforce (10)
Markington CE Primary School, Harrogate

Ocean

Shiny seaweed swishing across the rocks,
People collecting shells and sand,
Fish swimming in the rock pools,
Deep blue sea, dolphins, whales and sharks swimming
Down,
Down,
Down,
The night sky reflecting on the gentle ripples,
Waves crashing on the shore.

Lucy Bainbridge (8)
Markington CE Primary School, Harrogate

Dreams For The World

'I don't want to spread my diseases,'
Muttered the old rat.
'I don't want to destroy houses,'
Mumbled the earthquake.
'I don't want to go to Heaven,'
Cried the grandma.
'I want to be fresh and clean,'
Whispered the water.
'I don't want to kill anyone,'
Roared the rocket launcher.
'I don't want to leave Planet Earth,'
Said the people that live there.

Ben Coates (10)
Markington CE Primary School, Harrogate

War's Consequences

'Don't want to kill,'
Screamed the bullet.
'I don't want to leave war,'
Shouted the wounded soldier.
'Why is this happening to me?'
Shouted the rough ground of Afghanistan.
I'm not too sure about this,
Thought the brave soldier.
'Why did he go to war?'
Questioned the soldier's mum.
I wonder if my family are OK?
Thought the doctor in Afghanistan.

Joe Manock (9)
Markington CE Primary School, Harrogate

I Wanna Be

I wanna be a millionaire with a
Bright red, shimmering sports car,
Rushing to Hollywood pop stars
To see my friends.
I wanna be a vet, saving lives of
Poorly animals who are suffering.
I wanna be a writer with
Interesting books for children
With funny jokes and tales to tell.
I wanna be a diver to see
Beautiful dolphins swim in the sea,
Swimming next to me.

Rebekah Benson (10)
Markington CE Primary School, Harrogate

It's Just A Dream

'I want to be clean,'
Trickled the dirty water.
'I can only dream to have some money,'
Wished the poor housewife.
'It would be heaven if I was lived in,'
Sobbed the tin house.
'I wish to be full,'
Echoed the starved stomach.
'I don't want to run down the street,'
Gushed the sewers.
'I don't want to spread,'
Bellowed the illness.

Frances Houseman (11)
Markington CE Primary School, Harrogate

The Ocean

T he swooping seagulls
H orizon pink and red
E ver beautiful

O pen space
C rashing waves
E nchanting fish
A lways there
N ever-ending.

Ellie Simmerson (9)
Markington CE Primary School, Harrogate

The World Will Change

'I wish there was peace between countries and no wars,'
Cried the dying soldier.
'I wish everyone had a job who wants one,'
Sighed the unemployed worker.
'I want to be used,'
Murmured the neglected bike.
'I wish I had money for my family,'
Sobbed the moneyless mother.

John Houseman (10)
Markington CE Primary School, Harrogate

Space

Moon monster,
Star sparkler,
Planet player,
Sky shooter,
Rocket roarer,
Comet crasher,
Galaxy gobbler,
Alien attacker.

Oliver Houseman (9)
Markington CE Primary School, Harrogate

The Sea

T he sea crashes on the rocks
H ear the waves
E nchanting fish

S ometimes in, sometimes out
E verywhere creatures swim
A mazing, colourful sea life.

Bradley Peacock (8)
Markington CE Primary School, Harrogate

The Stepping Stones Of Life

First step:
A tiny baby, so delicate and sweet,
With a toothless grin
And minute hands and feet.

Second step:
A growing toddler, just learned to walk,
A sense of humour
And a squeaky little talk.

Third step:
A child who has red, rosy skin,
Loves to run around
And loves to win!

Fourth step:
An older teenager, getting more mature (maybe),
Whether or not
It carries on further.

Fifth step:
A fully grown adult, just ready to work,
They'd better get going,
There's no time to lurk.

Sixth step:
A grandparent now, has the time to sit and stare,
Likes to make you feel better,
They do it 'cause they care.

You will not want me to carry on
Because you know what happens,
They'll soon be gone.
So there's more to life than meets the eye,
As big grey stepping stones whistle by!

Maria Atwell (10)
St Aelred's RC Primary School, York

Pigs Galore

A pig is a pig,
Of that there's no doubt,
Sometimes they're big,
'Specially the snout.

Pigs galore,
Pigs galore,
Pigs, pigs, pigs, pigs,
Pigs galore.

They are dirty creatures
Around in the hay,
With special features,
Too much meat today.

Pigs galore,
Pigs galore,
Pigs, pigs, pigs, pigs,
Pigs galore.

Chop it to bacon,
Fry it in a pan,
Beef steak isn't taken,
Just avoid if you can.

Pigs galore,
Pigs galore,
Pigs, pigs, pigs, pigs,
Pigs galore.

You might have some sausage
With tomato sauce,
Stop taking cows hostage,
Use a pig of course.

Pigs galore,
Pigs galore,
Pigs, pigs, pigs, pigs,
Pigs galore.

Looking at pork,
It really is sweet,
But we're not here to talk,
We're here to eat.

Pigs galore,
Pigs galore,
Pigs, pigs, pigs, pigs,
Pigs galore.

Now I have to go,
To buy meat for a winner.
I'm never that slow,
Just enjoy your dinner.

Pigs galore,
Pigs galore,
Pigs, pigs, pigs, pigs,
Pigs galore.

Matty Graves (11)
St Aelred's RC Primary School, York

Snowflakes

S now falling endlessly
N othing stopping it
O ut in the freezing cold
W inter fun, fun, fun
F alling slowly
L aughing all day
A ll the kids having fun
K ind snowmen coming out
E veryone is out playing all day
S adness nowhere to be found.

Chad Hammerton (10)
St Aelred's RC Primary School, York

My Brother Threw A Snowball

My brother threw a snowball,
It hit me on the back.
When he threw the snowball,
It hit me with a *thwack*.

Throw, throw, *thwack, thwack,*
Thwack, thwack, throw, throw.

My brother threw a snowball,
It hit my mother's head.
When he threw the snowball,
She fell into the shed.

Throw, throw, *thwack, thwack,*
Thwack, thwack, throw, throw.

My brother threw a snowball,
It hit my friend, Tim.
When he threw the snowball,
We all ambushed him.

Ben Godfrey (11)
St Aelred's RC Primary School, York

Snow Is . . .

Snow is . . .
Rosy-red cheeks, like red cherries glowing,
Dry leaves, like crisps crackling,
Sharp icicles, like witches' fingernails stabbing,
Cold snow drops like cotton balls falling,
Snowflakes, like stars, sparkling.

Georgia Bowlby (10)
St Aelred's RC Primary School, York

The Fish

Hungry,
It sat there on Monday.

There it lay
On the cold Tuesday.

Then in May
It sat on a log on Wednesday.

In the Ouse
It was, on Thursday.

Finally it swam away
On a frosty Friday.

It was a . . . Zander!

Joshua Ogiela (11)
St Aelred's RC Primary School, York

The Sunrise Day

Early in the morning
A peacock stood perplexed and still,
Waiting for the sun to rise,
When a fox took him by surprise.
He could see his reflection
In the fox's eyes,
When suddenly a slithery snake
Sneakily slithered through the grass,
Shocking the fox into running away
And this was the beginning
Of the sunrise day.

Megan Robinson (9)
St Aelred's RC Primary School, York

Autumn

Autumn smells like pumpkin pie,
Autumn is breezy with winds very high.
Autumn is golden and yellow and red,
And I love autumn for the reasons I've said.

When I look at the trees the leaves are falling,
I look at the sky, the clouds are rolling.
The days are shorter, the nights are long,
And I love autumn as it rolls along.

Autumn is great - we can play in the leaves.
Autumn is cold - we can snug up as we please.
Autumn is heading for winter and my birthday is in November,
So now do you see why I love autumn?

Emelia Lawrence (7)
St Aelred's RC Primary School, York

Snow

Snow is . . .
Snowballs, like sparkly baubles, flying.
Roads, like ice, freezing.
Trees, like radiant icicles, twinkling.
Snowflakes, like bright disco balls, blinding.
Lamp posts, like gigantic bulbs, glowing.
Fire, like tender flames, crackling.
Cars, like gentle wind, moving.
Noses, like rosy cherries, crystallising.
Feet, like cold floors, shivering.

Kristof Gotts (10)
St Aelred's RC Primary School, York

Into The Night

Sneaking down the hall,
She crept upon the wooden floor.
She kept on doing this until
She reached the pure white door.

The key turned,
The handle bent,
She saw what she wanted to see,
The busy streets of Kent.

The wind was strong
The time was right
To suddenly creep
Into the night.

Jess Whitehead (10)
St Aelred's RC Primary School, York

Winter

Winter is . . .
Rosy-red cheeks, like hot apples,
Tumbling stars that hit the ground calmly,
Freezing children waiting patiently,
Glistening icicles shaped like daggers,
Glowing noses like Rudolph's,
Blankets of snow on the streets,
Sprinkles of sugar on a sponge cake.
That is winter!

George Wallace (11)
St Aelred's RC Primary School, York

Snow Is . . .

Snow is like a blinding blizzard
Gushing through the air.
Snow is like icing on a cake,
Covering all the rooftops.

Icicles are like frozen carrots
Hanging from a window sill.
Icicles are like stabbing daggers
Jingling together on the ceiling of a cave.

Cheeks are like glowing red cherries.
Cheeks are like Rudolph's nose,
So very rosy.

Dan Tingley (11)
St Aelred's RC Primary School, York

Frosty Days

It was a chilly, snowy day,
Even though it was the middle of May.
The snowflakes falling tens by tens,
In their shelters, chickens and hens.
Snowflakes tossing to and fro,
People not knowing where to go.
Snowmen being built, with scarves and hats,
Snow prints on the door mat.

Chloé Cawood (11)
St Aelred's RC Primary School, York

Winter Is . . .

Frozen blue icicles, like golden carrots, freezing.
Cold, flying wind, like white fans blowing.
Rosy red cheeks, like tasty cherries glowing.
Shiny snowballs, like small raindrops trickling.
Bright, sore noses, like sharp ice crystallising.
Big grey lamp posts, like a long light glistening.
Snowdrops fall, like cotton balls dropping.
Cold snowflakes, like stars twinkling.

Charlotte Davison (10)
St Aelred's RC Primary School, York

Snow

Snow,
Snowflakes,
Cold snowman, snowballs,
Children laughing and playing,
Children's wet clothes,
White ground,
All over.

Charlotte Grange (10)
St Aelred's RC Primary School, York

My Dog, Monty – Haiku

My Labradoodle
Has oddly only three legs,
But we still love him.

Fern Hawkridge (11)
St Aelred's RC Primary School, York

Winter Wonderland – Haiku

Going right outside
To build a pretty snowman.
I need a carrot.

Jodie Wortley (11)
St Aelred's RC Primary School, York

Winter Tree – Haiku

Branches like cobwebs,
Soft snow settles silently,
Soaring birds float by.

Thomas Morrison (10) & Paul Duke (11)
St Aelred's RC Primary School, York

Bang, Bang!

The wind whistles all around.
Suddenly there is a loud sound.
Bright colours make a smile,
Dimming into darkness.

Bang, bang,
They clap their hands,
Over and over again.

Sparklers spitting out
Their silver sparks
The smell of burning
As the bonfire roars.

Bang, bang,
They clap their hands
Over and over again.

Shooting up to the stars,
Stretching their wings
So they can fly.

Bang, bang,
They clap their hands
Over and over again.

Flinging their arms
Round and round,
Exploding on this very day
In the dark night sky.

Bang, bang,
They clap their hands
Over and over again.

Caitlin Eadie (10)

St George's RC Primary School, York

The River Nile

The river flows in and out,
Smooth and wild,
Flooding each year,
Which brings new life.
So powerful the river,
It cuts a nation in half.

You see the crops on black silt,
You see the joyful faces,
You see the water rush by,
You see the crops on black silt.

Across the river Kufu lies,
Hidden within great Giza.
Crocodiles hide beneath the waves,
Stalking their prey.

You see the crops in black silt,
You see the joyful faces,
You see the water rush by,
You see the crops in black silt.

The river opens its mouth,
Splitting in two.
He spits all the water out into the sea.
There you see the river end,
What a pleasant sight it is!

Jacob Dyer (11)
St George's RC Primary School, York

A Magical Winter

As autumn turns to winter,
The world turns frosty and freezing.
As the nights get dark early
And the trees become bare,
We see a big change.

When the tree branches move side to side,
We can hear the wind whistle in our ears.
We hear bonfires going *bang, bang, bang,*
Or the *crunch, crunch, crunch* of our
Footsteps on the snowy ground.

When we arrive home we may
Smell warm roast dinner.
Hot chocolate at market stalls
And chestnuts on street corners.

In the morning we may hold
A warm mug of tea,
Although if we are unlucky,
Maybe some cold, smooth ice.

When it starts to snow we can taste
The small white drops dissolve on our tongues.
A warm supper to eat or drink,
Until it is time for bed.

Erin O'Kane (10)
St George's RC Primary School, York

Please Help Me!

Please help me,
The sea is so big
And my boat is so small.

The waves crashing fiercely,
The sky getting grey.

Please help me,
The sea is so big
And my boat is so small.

The thunder, the lightning,
The rocking of my boat.

Please help me,
The sea is so big
And my boat is so small.

The fishing nets are empty,
The night is so cold.

Please help me,
The sea is so big
And my boat is so small.

Holly Walker (11)
St George's RC Primary School, York

Snow

Wow, it's snow!
It's cold,
It's sticky,
It's wet.

Wow, it's snow!
I can throw snowballs,
I can make snowmen,
I can sledge.

Wow, it's snow!
It looks like a carpet,
It sounds crunchy,
It dances as it falls.

Wow, it's snow!
I think it's quiet,
I think it's soft,
I think it's beautiful,

I love it!

Christian Roxburgh (7)
St George's RC Primary School, York

Mr Monsters

Monsters, monsters jumping
In your bedroom.
When you go to sleep
They give you a little fright,
So watch out for those monsters.

Nadine Mapplebeck (8)
St George's RC Primary School, York

Robin Hood

Robin Hood, Robin Hood,
Fighting with all his might.
He gets his arrows, he fights,
He always fights with might.

Robin Hood, Robin Hood,
He's very brave
And really good,
Arrows or might?

Robin Hood
Wears green.
He's the best,
Robin Hood!

Robin Hood
Who has an arrow
Called Silver Arrow,
His best arrow!
Robin Hood!

Kamila Kutna (10)
St George's RC Primary School, York

Dragons

Dragons are so scary.
Some of them are big
And some are little.
Dragons are so green
And they always breathe fire.

Michaela McVeagh (8)
St George's RC Primary School, York

A Walking Dream

I wake up once more to live my life again,
For then I realise how lucky I am
To live next to the riverside.
So I guzzle down my Coco Pops,
Put on my hat and coat,
My wellies I will never forget.
I say farewell to Mum and Dad
And open the door to a lovely breeze.
Such wonderful views I finally find.
The riverbank.
The reflection of me just can't see,
But one thing I know is that the fishes can.
The boats flow by with a calming smile,
Wishing me all the best,
For I will become a sailor.
The river is a wonderful place
To have a picnic at the grass bank.
I just know it!

Chloe Neill (11)

St George's RC Primary School, York

Snow

Snow is white,
What a sweet sight.
Snow is cold,
But it's not for the old.
Mother Nature is so kind
To put snow into my mind.

Joseph Iggulden (8)

St George's RC Primary School, York

The Aston Martin DBS

I scream along the track
Making things a blur.
My engine is revving to go,
But when I shoot off it emits nothing but a purr.

You'll be lucky if you catch me,
I'll be gone in a flash.
I have to watch other things coming,
Or I'll collide with a *bash!*

The sun shines on me,
It makes me glorious and bright.
My paintwork is amazing
When it flashes in the light.

Now put them together,
If you guess wrong I won't think less.
Fine, I think I'll tell you then,
I'm the Aston Martin DBS.

Sam Lightfoot-Loftus (10)
St George's RC Primary School, York

Walking In The Woods

I walk slowly through the woods,
Turning and swirling.
In the deep mist
There are tall trees and short grass.
I listen to the echoing birds.
I'm too amazed, and lost for words.

Louis Brown (10)
St George's RC Primary School, York

My Horse And Me

My horse and me are like best friends,
Always there for each other.
She's beautiful, brave and loyal,
To her I'm like a mother.

She has fur of shining ebony,
And eyes that search for me.
A tail made of pure silk.
That blows in the summer breeze.

When we ride in meadows and valleys,
She whinnies with happiness and glee.
Her long mane blows in the soft wind,
There we will always be free.

We will always be together,
To her we are a family.
Always, forever,
My horse and me.

Katy Staite (10)
St George's RC Primary School, York

Horses

Horses, horses,
Soft nose in the middle of your hand.
Trotting up and down
On the saddle.
Sweet, sweet horses!

Alana Loughrey (8)
St George's RC Primary School, York

Space

Planets, stars and moons . . .
More discovered soon.
All up in the sky,
Further than we could fly.

Spaceships in the air,
They will have a scare,
When they land on Mars
And find life that's not ours.

Through the dark black sky
Unmanned spaceships fly,
Looking at the sun,
That job must *not* be fun!

In space stations men will
Live like they were still
On the Earth and safe,
And not in outer space!

Harriet Fewster (9)
St George's RC Primary School, York

Cats

Cats, cats, wonderful cats,
Playing, scratching, miaowing, biting,
Licking milk, milk, milk,
Wonderful cats.
Miaow! Miaow! Cats.

Jaime Rodgers-Gray (8)
St George's RC Primary School, York

Robin Hood

Help lender,
Fight mender,
Rich taker,
Love maker,
Poor giver,
Never quiver,
Gloom fighter,
Moon lighter,
Light bringer,
Life healer.

He is so clever
He will live forever.
He is very, very bold
And his story will be ever told.
He is good
And it's *Robin Hood!*

Julietta Dodd (9)
St George's RC Primary School, York

Animals

A is for animals scampering around
N is for night sky where bats fly high
I is for island where wild beasts live
M is for monkeys who live in the trees
A is for apples the animals eat
L is for lakes where fish swim around
S is for snakes that slither in the trees.

Hattie Snaith (9)
St George's RC Primary School, York

February's First Ball

As I kneel down,
Scraping the whiteness from all around,
I form it in my hands cupped,
Whilst I pat it and tap it, making it round.

I check over my shoulder as I sit on my knees,
Watching the target as he stands in the breeze,
Adding more snow to make it more round.

I hold it up high, admiring the shape,
February's first ball, so perfectly round!
I pull back my arm, then throw hard as I can,
February's first ball flies through the air!

Smack! It hits my target straight on his back!
He screams my name, I hear through my laughter and tears,
And then it begins - the snowball fight of the year!

Rosie Garvey-Cocker (9)
St George's RC Primary School, York

Who Am I?

I play for Liverpool FC,
I play for England FC,
I wear number 4, England FC,
I am one of the best players in the world.
I love to be the captain.
I wear number 8 for Liverpool FC.
Who am I?

A: I am Gerrard!

Jamie Frary (10)
St George's RC Primary School, York

Emotions

I am something you cannot control,
Something that everyone has.
Whether falling in love
Or raging with anger,
I'm still the same old me.
I've been around for thousands of years
Controlling people's minds.
I can be happy, sad, anything you like,
I could be furious,
I could be excited as well as vicious,
I'm the feeling inside you,
The burning fire inside your heart,
The feeling that's still alive,
The heart that never dies,
The emotions inside you all.

Audrey Chishinge (11)
St George's RC Primary School, York

A Mother

A mother is something that you can't buy.
She is loving, caring, sharing and kind,
She always keeps an eye.
She is always there when you need her,
She picks you up when you are down.
You can tell her your secret
Because you know you can trust her.
A mother is always there in good and bad t mes,
So be grateful that you have a mother who loves you.

Tino Chigeza (10)
St George's RC Primary School, York

The Throne And The Stone

King Tutankhamun
Had a tomb
Built from bricks
And piled up sticks.
One slave said,
'Let's go to bed,'
But with a swing of an axe
At its very max,
He had lost his head,
He was dead.
Tutankhamun said,
'I'll keep the throne
And you'll have the stone.'

Motto: Don't mess with the king.

John Carlyle (9)
St George's RC Primary School, York

Robin Hood

R escuer
O ver-powerful
B old
I nvincible
N oble

H appy
O ptimistic
O ld
D ead.

Henry van Dijk (10)
St George's RC Primary School, York

The Man In The Wood

A man who's caring
And he's daring.

A man with arrows,
Who cries over his sorrows.

A man who's fearless
And he's not careless.

A good man,
Whose name isn't Sam.

A man who steals from the rich,
And I can assure you this isn't a glitch.

A man whose name is Robin Hood,
And he lived in a forest called Sherwood.

Joseph Hill (10)
St George's RC Primary School, York

Robin Hood

Robin
Hood in the
wood. Saving people
everywhere, even if it
is a dare. He's helpful
and kind, he helps the blind.
He breaks the law to feed the
poor. He looks ahead for the dead.
You may think he's kind but he's a
killer in my mind.

Hattie Falgate (9)
St George's RC Primary School, York

Advent

You swap your things in a market,
The No.1 shop is their target.
Is there a present that doesn't go well?
Is there a present that won't sell?
Fancy wrapping you will adore,
You will not be a bore.
Now to get this serious,
Time to stop this silliness,
Christmas is a time for Christ, not play.
Christ should not be delayed.
Yet if God had not given so,
No one would know him from top to toe.
He would never have been
The baby in the manger.

Princess Nomqhele Ndlazulwana (8)
St George's RC Primary School, York

Robin Hood

There once was a man called Robin Hood
Who lived in a forest called Sherwood,
With his merry men, Gary, the almighty,
John, the skilful,
Bill, the fighter,
Ben, the thinker,
Robin, the almighty, the skilful, the fighter and the thinker.
Robin didn't understand the word 'impossible'.
He would not stop fighting for days and nights
Till he had won the fight.

Roberto Henderson (10)
St George's RC Primary School, York

Tears

The tears,
They're creeping quietly,
Closing in on me,
Just welling up inside me.
It was just pure luck that he
Appreciated my so-called 'beauty',
Although I should have attached myself to him.
This is the worst mistake I could have made.
How could I have lost my engagement ring?
He doesn't believe that I lost it,
He ignores me.
All my focus has blurred.
The first tear creeps down my face . . .

Georgina Dodd (10)
St George's RC Primary School, York

Winter's Snow

Swirling round,
Pearl-white and cold,
It crunches under my feet,
I'm in a wonderland,
Dancing through snow.
I am like an artist at work,
But the canvas is melting quickly.
Individual shapes come fluttering and floating
Down to my rescue,
Worry-free until reality comes flooding back.
My work is done, I must leave.

Evie Jackson (10)
St George's RC Primary School, York

Torres!

Torres, Torres he is a red,
Scoring goals for Liverpool, the best.
The more he scores the crowd roars
And he celebrates like heck!

Torres, Torres he is the best,
33 goals last season,
That's as good as he gets.
No one will beat the best!

Torres puts his boots on
And the Kop breaks into song.
A person to please the crowd,
The Kop roars and he scores all day long!

Patrick Wintie (10)
St George's RC Primary School, York

Blue Trousers

Blue trousers,
Blue trousers,
I've seen a boy wearing blue trousers.
Not black, not green,
Not red, not orange.
The sun above
When you don't need a scarf,
You don't need a hat.
Blue trousers,
Blue trousers,
Who's that boy wearing blue trousers?

Ross Garvey-Cocker (7)
St George's RC Primary School, York

The Goalkeeper

Standing in the goal
Feeling really cold,
Diving to the left,
Diving to the right,
Giving my all
To stop that ball.
Jumping up high,
Stretching down low,
Shot's coming in,
Where will it go?
Got to catch it
To get that win.

Jack Bell (11)
St George's RC Primary School, York

Max!

Max is as small as a pageboy suit,
But he is as fast as a newt.
He is as clumsy as a truck,
But can make noises like a duck.
He's as soft as a big green chair,
Belonging in a spider's lair.
Max is a bit of a chortler,
But he loves water.
Max is like a saxophone,
But speaks like a church dome.
He's the one who wants a sax,
That's my brother, *Max!*

Tim Wilson (10)
St George's RC Primary School, York

Robin Hood

Robin is as courageous as a wolf.
If you ever see him, you would
Think that you're in Heaven.
He's generous and helpful,
He won't let you down.

He is like a sneaky magpie
Preying on the rich to feed the poor.
He would never let you down.

He puts people before himself.
He's brave, he's bold and he's fearless.
He would never let you down.

Shanahan Rai
St George's RC Primary School, York

Star

The star shines bright in the sky,
So far away up, up high.

Comes out at night
And makes our path bright.

It is pearly white
And is a lovely sight.

There are millions of them up there
In the high, misty air.

They start shining at the end of the day,
Ready to light a traveller's way.

Joshua Wilson
St George's RC Primary School, York

Fireworks

F ireworks, fireworks, they are great
I love seeing them soar into the sky
R ockets rushing into the air
E veryone loves fireworks
W hat a sight
O ur fireworks twirl in the sky
R ockets are roaring
K ind they are, giving us a show
S oaring fireworks in the sky.

In all different colours, people love fireworks.
Remember the 5th of November.

Daisy Dyrdal-Mortimer (11)
St George's RC Primary School, York

What A Difference

A nts are tiny, black, little things, not even as big as a bug! But
N ewts are silly dragons and
I guanas are so scaly. Iguanas are also quiet and dry, unlike
M onkeys who jabber all the time. Monkeys are funny, furry
fluff balls swinging in the trees.
A nteaters are different again with their long tongues and
diet of ants.
L lamas are most different by far; timid, so loving trees.

These are only a few of
The animals in our great world.
Wouldn't you like to be one too?

Mary Willis (10)
St George's RC Primary School, York

Monsters

Monsters,
Monsters are so scary,
Some are green,
Some are hairy.
Some breathe fire,
Some can fly,
Very high,
But the ones you can't see,
They are the scariest for me!

Niall Huggins (8)
St George's RC Primary School, York

Dinosaurs!

D inosaurs
I ntelligent
N oisy
O ld
S tegosaurus
A crobatic
U gly
R oaring
S o cool!

Connor Trueman
St George's RC Primary School, York

Christmas

C is for Christ
H is for holly that hangs on your door
R is for a reindeer
I is for ice that comes when it's cold
S is for Santa, who gives you presents
T is for tree that you put up
M is for merry, everyone is this at Christmas
A is for angels, they are God's messengers
S is for snow.

Clare Willis (8)
St George's RC Primary School, York

Fruity

Strawberries are red, blueberries are blue,
I like cherries, so do you!
Bananas are sweet, oranges are sour,
You always need fruit to give you power!

Strawberries are red, blueberries are blue,
I like cherries, so do you!
So remember all of your five-a-day,
And always keep the healthy way!

Anna O'Donnell (10)
St George's RC Primary School, York

The Wind

Who has seen the wind?
Neither I nor you,
But when the leaves hang trembling,
The wind is passing through.

Who has seen the wind?
Neither you nor I,
But when the trees bow down their heads
The wind is passing by.

Donald Chimalilo (8)
St George's RC Primary School, York

The Moon And Stars

The moon and the stars in space,
Mercury and Venus are so ace.
There is no gravity so you'll definitely float,
And you will not survive unless you have a space coat.

There is never a day, it is always night.
When you get home it will be so bright.
After all of that you have to go home
And you find another fascinating adventure in Rome.

Patrick Foster (10)
St George's RC Primary School, York

Nature

All the leaves fall down
In the city town.
Flowers in the woods,
Some are still in their buds.

Birds in their nests,
Bumblebees are the best.
All the green, green grass,
As you can hear the bass.

George Vardy (8)
St George's RC Primary School, York

My Feelings

Sometimes I feel sad
Because I have been bad.
Sometimes I feel happy
Because I have had a drink from the tappy.

Sometimes I feel angry
Because I have had no tangy.
Sometimes I feel amazed
Because I have been offered an act on the stage.

Matthew Sayer (9)
St George's RC Primary School, York

The Shadow

There it stood, deep in the shadows dark
Beneath the trees in the ancient park.
Midnight struck and I heard a voice,
'The Earth's command is at your choice.'
I knocked on the door, trembling with fright,
For I wasn't alone, it was the dead of night.
A phantom shadow, I believe I see,
A terrifying voice has spoken to me.

Azia Carlyle (10)
St George's RC Primary School, York

Robin Hood

He's brave, he's strong and mighty,
He steals from the rich to save the poor.
He's kind and caring,
Clever, and will be for evermore.
Where there's danger, he will be there
With his merry men.
They're sneaky, fast, clever and cool.
All together they rule.

Jordan Benjamin-Sutton (10)
St George's RC Primary School, York

My Daddy

My daddy is a comfy leather sofa, cuddly and welcoming.
My dad is a blue submarine, fast and a great swimmer.
My dad is like a school desk, always on the ball.
My dad is a shiny silver star, bright and understanding.
My dad is like a muscleman, strong and energetic.
My dad is an Ipswich football top, sporty and fun.
But most of all my dad is a fluffy pink heart,
Loving, caring, funny and the best dad in the whole wide *world!*

Imogen Wood (10)
St George's RC Primary School, York

Robin Hood

Robin Hood is so brave
He could fight three people at a time
And he would still win.
Robin Hood, you are the best,
No one can beat you.
Robin Hood, you are good,
You steal from the rich to feed the poor
And get on the wrong side of the sheriff's law.

Ben Harris (9)
St George's RC Primary School, York

Snow

Snow is white,
Snow is crumbly
But it's also lovely.
Soft and cold on my hands.
Falling from the sky
Onto my head.
Snowflakes
Making patterns on my coat.

Tilly Brown (7)
St George's RC Primary School, York

The Sea

Down in the depths of the deep blue sea
There's a giant squid waiting for me.
He's big, lonely and enormously fat,
In the hold of the shipwreck is where he is sat.
Now on the other side of the world in the freezing ocean
There's someone else doing the locomotion.
They're furry, cute and very dangerous.
It's a polar bear.

Michael Silver (11)
St George's RC Primary School, York

The Boy

There once was a boy who always peeked,
Everyone called him a geek.
He was going to the shop
To buy a fizzy pop.
He went to Greece
To see his cousin, Reece.
A girl came and she asked for a cake
Before he visited the lake.

Bijay Gurung
St George's RC Primary School, York

Doctor Who

Once there was a doctor
And he had an enemy called Miss Foster.
He had an enemy called the Dalek
And he is smart and the doctor thought he was made of plastic.
He has a friend called Rose,
And she does owe people loads of money.
The Cyberman is a great enemy, but he is a dummy.
I am the doctor and can say, *'Wahoo!'*

Bailey Kinley (8)
St George's RC Primary School, York

Animals

Dolphins, dolphins, they're sweet,
When they're good you give them a treat.
Horses, horses, they're good to you,
Like a cow that goes *moo, moo.*
Birds, birds in the sky,
Some fly low and some fly high.
Monkeys, monkeys, they're so cool,
They can even swim in a pool.

Celine Carter (9)
St George's RC Primary School, York

The Fire

The fire is hot.
Red, orange flames
Flicker and dance.
Scary but exciting
Inferno.

Lewis Ewan (7)
St George's RC Primary School, York

Dragons

Scaly,
Crashing, flying, fire-bashing,
Terrifying, evil, fire-breathing
Monsters.
Argh!

Agata Hodur (8)
St George's RC Primary School, York

Thunderstorm

Trees rustle in the howling wind.
Bang! Crash! Rumble!
Goes the thunder when it's crashing.
Lightning flashes, lighting up the misty moor.
Rain comes pouring - pouring - pouring
Down to the misty moor.

Bang! Kaboom! Crash!
Goes the thunder, still carrying on.
Trees get struck to the floor
Like a person tripping up.
Thunder bangs, lightning strikes and wind howls.
Storms are a man's fear.

Lightning flickers like a candle on a misty night.
Thunder bangs like a set of drums.
Wind howls like a grey wolf.
All of a sudden the lightning disappears,
The thunder calms and the wind drops.
Peace in our world.

Gwyn Owen (8)
St Joseph's Catholic Primary School, Harrogate

Crash

As the bushes are lying, lying, lying,
The storm is drawing nigh.
Now the storm is here and
The lightning strikes the trees,
So hard that it would electrocute you,
Giving you an astonishing reaction.
The trees go falling, falling, falling
Down to the ground.

The lightning is like veins
Being drawn in the sky,
As light as a candle.
The lightning thrashes,
Falling trees, falling leaves.

Gusty winds slashing the bushes,
They're like a farmer,
Whipping, whipping, whipping a corner.
Thunder sounds like the big bass drums.
The storm is over.

Olivia Cook (7)
St Joseph's Catholic Primary School, Harrogate

Thunderstorm

Thunderstorm lashes down on gusty trees
And lightning strikes back,
Warning everyone to go back
Before lightning strikes back.
Boom! Bang! Crash! Crack!

Rain lashes down on the grass.
Suddenly all the trees go *whoosh!*
Lightning strikes quicker - quicker - quicker -
Quicker down to the ground . . .
Crash! Boom! Bang! Crash!
Boom! Bang! . . . Crack!

Cormac Flanagan (7)
St Joseph's Catholic Primary School, Harrogate

Thunder Cracks!

Thunder cracks in the gusty storm,
Just like a building has been hit by an enormous boulder . .
Bang! The next night will be another night of *doom!*

The wind is a gusty galleon
Tossed upon the rustling trees.
Whoosh! The reaction on the people is big.

The rain is lashing down, down, down,
Along with the hailstones,
Just like a lot of meteors hitting the earth. *Boom!*
Forests fear when lightning comes near.

Edward Ostler (8)
St Joseph's Catholic Primary School, Harrogate

Crash, Boom, Bang!

As the lightning strikes
The trees shudder with fear.
The thunder, *bang, bang, bangs!*
Lightning is coming over here,
Crackling noises are echoing,
Crash, boom, bang!

Grey clouds are approaching,
Sparks falling nigh like a sparkler on Bonfire Night.
The trees are falling, falling, falling.
Crash, boom, bang!

Emily Timson (8)
St Joseph's Catholic Primary School, Harrogate

Stormy Night!

The wind goes *whoosh* in the misty, stormy night.
The lightning crackles like fireworks lighting up the sky.
The thunder roars like a drum, booming louder, louder,
Louder in the dark, misty night.
The lightning catches the trees and they go falling,
Falling, falling down to the ground and go *crash!*
The lightning lights up the sky and goes *crack!*
The wind blows the snow all around.
What a stormy night!

Caitlin Smith (8)
St Joseph's Catholic Primary School, Harrogate

Thunderstorm

Trees crashing, thunder cackling
In the night of the *thunderstorm!*
Blinding lightning, howling, howling ghost
In the night of the *thunderstorm!*
In the night sky it is like roaring dragons
Crashing in the night sky.
Bang, bang, boo it goes.
I am not lying. This time the
Thunderstorm is right in front of you!

Sarah Maxwell (7)
St Joseph's Catholic Primary School, Harrogate

War Of The Roses

Henry the VII
Won the battle of Bosworth
Sad, sad Richard died

King Richard III
Was the boss of the white rose
Henry's men killed him

He found a gold crown
In a prickly thorn bush
The new king, Henry.

Jack Love & Nathan Higgins (8)
Sutton Park Primary School, Hull

The Deathbed Series Of Henry VIII – Haikus

Parr was widowed soon,
Fat Henry was dead at last!
It's sad, but lucky.

Some happy at last,
Younger heir to the old throne,
Except for right now . . .

Henry is gone now,
My son to the throne at last!
Edward, do my job.

Macy Wiles & Jessica Smith (9)
Sutton Park Primary School, Hull

The War Of The Roses

Henry VII,
The great war of the roses,
Fought in a battle.

Armies shocked to death,
Arrows shooting all the time,
Henry killed Richard.

King Richard was *dead,*
Henry stabbed him in the leg.
The end of the war!

Harvey Marritt & Jarrod Scott (9)
Sutton Park Primary School, Hull

The War Of The Roses

Henry killed Richard
Soldiers pulled him from his horse
Arrows and armour

Horses and weapons
Red rose versus the white rose
Henry became king . . .

Samuel Smith (9) & Alex Sexton
Sutton Park Primary School, Hull

The Youngest King

Edward's mum was dead,
His dad was Henry VIII,
He was a good king.

He was really ill,
He died on his own big bed.
Poor, poor, poor Edward.

Callum Lane & Jordan Hutchinson (8)
Sutton Park Primary School, Hull

The War Of The Roses

Henry VII
Killed King Richard III!
Fire exploding . . .

Red rose and white rose . . .
Henry married Elizabeth,
Henry became king!

Alexander Morris & Ashley Ferguson (9)
Sutton Park Primary School, Hull

Henry VIII's Wives

He executed
Unlucky Katherine Howard.
She had a boyfriend!

Lucky Katherine Parr,
He did not chop off her head,
Because he was dead . . .

Mikyla Dillon (8) & Ellie Spence (9)
Sutton Park Primary School, Hull

Henry VIII And His Six Wives

Henry VIII was a big fat man,
Stuck his face in a frying pan.
Two wives lost their heads,
Anne Boleyn, Kathryn Howard
Got the big, black chop.

Tom Cracknell & Joshua Swain (9)
Sutton Park Primary School, Hull

Roller Coaster

Body shaking,
Tummy aching,
Train coming,
Heart dying,

Belts bang,
Slowly up,
Shooting down,
Quickly up,
Sharp turnings,
Head spinning,
Dizzy body,
Scream with laughter,
Coaster swirling,
Back to the entrance,

Off again.

Oliver Morris (10)
Thorpe Willoughby Community Primary School, Selby

Roller Coaster!

Fear

Butterflies emerging,
Heart thumping,
Sweat dripping,
Bars dropping,
Hands shaking.

Excitement

Belly dropping,
Hand waving,
Loud screaming,
Head banging,
Camera flashing.

Relief

Bars opening,
Heavy breathing,
Head aching,
Picture buying,
Sigh of relief.

Ellie Appleton (9)
Thorpe Willoughby Community Primary School, Selby

Roller Coaster

Electrifying

Head spinning,
Spine tingling,
Blood racing,
Heart pounding,
People screaming.

Fear

Stomach churning,
Eyes stinging,
Adrenalin pumping,
Completely thrilling,
Neck aching.

Hayden Stringer (10)
Thorpe Willoughby Community Primary School, Selby

Stig!

Fast driver,
Suit wearer,
Morse speaker,
Rain hater,
First successor,
Helmet bearer,
Mysterious character . . .
My hero!

Jack Head (9)
Tickton CE Primary School, Beverley

The Lonely, Romantic Fish

Always ready for a date
That will never occur,
She has never had a mate,
This really matters to her.

She swims around her tank
So, so gracefully,
Though to be completely frank,
Is she swimming happily?

Long, thin and purple-pink,
Masked in make-up all the time,
Her life has started to sink.
Her tail's the colour of lovely lime.

Ian White (10)
Tickton CE Primary School, Beverley

My Horse

Fence jumper,
Hay sleeper,
Run lover,
Trough eater,
Strong guardian,
Cow hater,
A good friend.

Isaac Galloway (8)
Tickton CE Primary School, Beverley

Future

F lying cars
U niverses of metal
T omorrow's world today
U nreal to the mortal eye
R un the race of time
E ndless action around me.

Phoebe Dickinson (9)
Tickton CE Primary School, Beverley

Doctor Who

D alek destroyer
R ose was his companion

W here will he end up next?
H ow does he defeat the aliens?
O h how his sonic screwdriver buzzes and unlocks doors.

Toby Redman (8)
Tickton CE Primary School, Beverley

Snowflakes Are So Beautiful

Snowflakes float gently from the sky,
Slowly they fall, passing by.

Twirling and whirling where they might,
Millions of snowflakes in flight.

Down, down, they go,
Blanketing the ground with so much snow.

Going where they may,
On the ground they lay.

Covering all that is bad,
Hiding all that is sad.

Ross Carrington (11)
Tilbury Primary School, Hull

Winter

Snowy winter, as cold as ice,
A sheet of snow lays on the ground.
Snow will fall from the sky.
The snow will melt and soon
It will turn into ice.
People will slide and slip,
Kids and people will play in the snow.

Bradley Kerswill (10)
Tilbury Primary School, Hull

The Snow

Snowflakes gently fall from the crystal-white sky,
Twisting and turning, as many children watch its beautiful luxuries.
As the gentle flakes form together, children excitedly
Wait for the huge white blanket to fall down at their feet.

The blanket has come.
The children are playing.
Laid on the ground, angels of snow are resting
As they watch the children in their comfort.

The clumped-up flakes are being grabbed by a large number of hands,
Turned into snowballs ready to join the fight.
One side wins, one side loses,
But all are happy about the wonderful delights of snow.

After the fight, snow is being rolled,
Rolled and rolled and rolled.
The children get spare hats, scarves and gloves
To put on the jolly snowmen.

The fun day is over,
Time to go inside,
Sit down in the big armchair
And relax with a cup of hot chocolate.

Caleb Devonport (10)
Woodthorpe Primary School, York

My Little Puppy Dog

My little puppy dog loves to bark,
All day long and all night long.
I walk him to the park
With him barking by my side.
I love to play with my little puppy dog,
He runs round and round,
He gets dizzier and dizzier.
My mum says to be more careful with him,
But I don't care and he doesn't care.
We take good care of each other.
I feed him twice a day.
He chews my shoes then he gets told off.
I feel sorry for him, he is only a puppy.

Chloe Wynn (7)
Woodthorpe Primary School, York

My Brother

My brother is a:
Mess maker,
Biscuit taker,
Hair brusher,
Pea musher,
Fast walker,
Boring talker,
Football player,
Lie sayer,
Nose picker,
Lolly licker.

Alicia Askew (9)
Woodthorpe Primary School, York

Naughty Kids, Good Kids

Naughty kids
Run around the place.
Good kids
Do what they are told to do.
Naughty kids,
Will they ever stop?
Good kids
Do what they are asked.
Naughty kids,
Where are you?
Good kids
Don't do what naughty kids do.

Caitlan Myers (7)
Woodthorpe Primary School, York

Magical Wands

There are four wands,
They are magical,
They make things appear.
You make spells with them.
Fairies use wands.
We played a game
With one naughty girl
With magic in it.
Books I made as magic books,
Made friends which were pretend.
They are very sparkly,
With magic in the air.

Georgia Coop (8)
Woodthorpe Primary School, York

The Seaside

T he waves crash against the wall
H eaps of sand on the shore
E at and drink a warm hot chocolate and fish with chips

S hells spread out on the shore
E at a nice warm meal
A ll the children playing in the sea
S ea's waves are as big as mountains
I see buckets and spades for everyone
D amp footprints on the steps
E at and have a nice cosy time.

Bethany Dobson (7)
Woodthorpe Primary School, York

Dreams Really Do Come True!

I once had a friend, I won't say her name,
But she thought every dream would come true next day.
Once she said she went up to space,
Next she thought she'd won a million-pound game of Ace,
So one day I told her, 'All these things you tell me,
They're just dreams,' I said.
Then she said, 'No they're not, I'll prove it!' So she did.
The next day she came along with three aliens
And a million pound cheque,
So I thought, *dreams really can come true!*

Aimee Robinson (9)
Woodthorpe Primary School, York

My Friend

My friend's crazy and never stops,
She likes to jump and skip and hop.
My friend's like an excited puppy,
She likes to jump in mud and get mucky.
My friend's mad but she doesn't care,
She likes being with you and she's always there.
My friend's favourite colour is pink,
She likes lemonade as it's her favourite drink.
My friend's cheeky and very messy,
Yep, you've guessed it. Her name is Jessie!

Rhian Pocock (9)
Woodthorpe Primary School, York

Happiness

Happiness is when I go on my bike.
Happiness is when I get presents.
Happiness is when I go to my grandma's.
Happiness is when I get sweets and chocolate.
Happiness is when I spend time with my family.
Happiness is when I see my pets.
Happiness is when I go on holiday.
Happiness is when I go to Center Parcs.
Happiness is when I go to see my friends in Norwich.
Happiness is when I see my friends.

Ruby Loftus (8)
Woodthorpe Primary School, York

Animals

Cheetah,
Fast and furious,
Sprinting
Through the jungle.

Horse,
Wild and free,
Galloping
Towards the sun.

These are my favourite animals.

Natasha Askew (11)
Woodthorpe Primary School, York

A Poem

Leaves blowing in the frost
Like confetti at a wedding.
A puppy snuffling in piles of leaves
Like a hedgehog in his bedding.
Leaves in the meadow all colours,
Like pillows from bedding.
Leaves are all colours,
Often green, brown, yellow, orange,
Like a piece of orange fruit.

Autumn Holmes (10)
Woodthorpe Primary School, York

My Family

My dad is a panther hunting for his prey.
My mum is a cheetah, rushing around the house.
My brother is a giraffe because he's very tall.
My sister is a bird, flying gracefully in the sky.
My nana is a bat, not knowing what to say.
My grandad is an elephant, really scared of mice.
My friends are crazy monkeys, always hanging round,
And I am a lonely rabbit locked up in a cage.

Chloe Muggeridge (9)
Woodthorpe Primary School, York

Blue

The sky is blue upon a sunny day
As the lush waves crash away.
My eyes are blue,
That's why I love you.
Blue is the colour of happiness
Upon a summer's day.
All the water from the swimming pool
Splashing away . . .

Scarlett Harris (9)
Woodthorpe Primary School, York

Animals

Monkey,
Small and cheeky
Hanging in the trees.

Cat,
Small and lazy,
Stretches under the tree.

These are my favourite animals.

Charlotte Lowther (11)
Woodthorpe Primary School, York

Slow And Fast

Slow,
Calm, careful,
Delayed, leisurely, straggle,
Let's slow it down, let's speed it up,
Sprinting, spanking, lively,
Brisk, rapid,
Fast.

Katie Cammidge (11)
Woodthorpe Primary School, York

Summer And Winter

Summer,
Warm, joyful,
Playing, rushing, running,
The warm summer, the cold winter,
Freezing, spreading, creeping,
Long, icy,
Winter.

Jessica Chadwick (10)
Woodthorpe Primary School, York

Dark And Light

Dark,
Murky, peaceful,
Cheerless, sombre, gloomy,
Gloomy as a grave, bright as a sun,
Blazing, glittering, gleaming,
Clear, bright,
Light.

Jarod Sellars (11)
Woodthorpe Primary School, York

Sky And Earth

Sky,
Unpredictable, brilliant,
Sparkling, boiling, blue-drenched,
Sky gives this to us, Earth gives this to us,
Gloomy, crumbling, drying,
Day, dirt,
Earth.

Matthew Parker (10)
Woodthorpe Primary School, York

Friends And Enemies

Friends,
Kind, joyful,
Playing, loving, hugging,
Friends stay together, enemies never ever,
Kicking, punching, bullying,
Unkind, mean,
Enemies.

Shannon Bryszkiewski (11)
Woodthorpe Primary School, York

Slow And Fast

Slow,
Calm, peaceful,
Careful, sluggish, dawdling,
The speed of a snail, the speed of light,
Bolt, supersonic, express,
Blurred, tiring,
Fast.

Sean Flatley (11)
Woodthorpe Primary School, York

Space

S pace is a forgotten galaxy waiting to be explored
P luto, Saturn, Mars
A shooting star
C omets flying
E ventually back home.

Amy Baker (10)
Woodthorpe Primary School, York

Black

Black is the colour of darkness.
Black is the colour in my eyes when I'm asleep.
Black is the colour of the night sky.
Black is my mum's favourite colour.
Black is the colour when you . . . die.

Charlotte Knight (10)
Woodthorpe Primary School, York

Jungle

A jungle is a noisy place,
Animals roaring, birds singing.
Animals eat and chomp, enjoying the food.
They sleep and eat all day long.

Ryan Wilson (8)
Woodthorpe Primary School, York

Seaside

Seaside, sea, wavy,
Sandcastles are everywhere,
Sand, soft and grainy.

Thomas Wrigglesworth (10)
Woodthorpe Primary School, York

Young Writers Information

We hope you have enjoyed reading this book - and that you will continue to enjoy it in the coming years.

If you like reading and writing poetry drop us a line, or give us a call, and we'll send you a free information pack.

Alternatively if you would like to order further copies of this book or any of our other titles, then please give us a call or log onto our website at www.youngwriters.co.uk

Young Writers Information
Remus House
Coltsfoot Drive
Peterborough
PE2 9JX
(01733) 890066